REORGANIZATION AND REFORM IN THE SOVIET ECONOMY

REORGANIZATION AND REFORM IN THE SOVIET ECONOMY

Edited by
Susan J. Linz and William Moskoff

M. E. Sharpe, Inc. Armonk, New York, and London

For our parents
Joe and Cora Johnston
Morris and Ann Moskoff

Second Printing

Copyright © 1988 by the Association for Comparative Economic
Studies.

Available in the United Kingdom and Europe from M. E. Sharpe,
Publishers, 3 Henrietta Street, London WC2E 8LU.

Library of Congress Cataloging-in-Publication Data

Reorganization and reform in the Soviet economy.

    Includes bibliographical references.

    1. Soviet Union—Economic policy—1986–   .
2. Soviet Union—Economic policy.   I. Linz, Susan J.
II. Moskoff, William.
HC 336.26.R46   1988   338.947   87–35630
ISBN 0-87332-472-2

Printed in the United States of America

Contents

Introduction

A spectre is haunting the Soviet Union—the spectre of economic stagnation.

It has been sixty years since central planning was instituted in the Soviet Union. This time period can be divided almost equally into thirty years of high and sustained growth and thirty years of a significant slowdown that has brought the Soviet Union to this critical moment in its history. Today economic reform is not a luxury championed by those who fear the consequences of inaction, nor is it even a ''useful'' thing to do to help the Soviet economy escape from its torpor. Reform is a crying necessity. Here is a society capable of putting men into space but not of producing a decent two-slice toaster, and whose jaded citizens often seek relief outside the law or inside a bottle.

To the helm of this society has come the first General Secretary of the Communist Party of the Soviet Union who was not alive at the time of the October Revolution. It is clear that, compared with his predecessors, he has much less of a vested interest in old institutions; indeed, he wants to remake the Soviet Union in an image that is in many ways utterly at odds with the existing order.

During his first two years in office, Gorbachev's reform proposals all fell within the framework of the traditional Soviet system of centralized planning and management of the economy. They were introduced as ways of improving the operation of central planning (through changes of personnel, reorganization of ministries and enterprises, changes in investment policy, campaign to raise labor discipline, minor revisions of income incentive systems), not of replacing that system.

A version of this introduction, along with the essays that follow, appeared in *Comparative Economic Studies*, Vol. 29, no. 4.

There is a strong conservative element in the Soviet Union that places high priority on allegiance to the existing institutions, including central planning.[1] Even within the reform camp, there is conflict.[2] Among those favoring change, for example, one finds support both for increasing centralization and for decentralization of decision-making in production and distribution. To be sure, those calling for reform are not necessarily calling for a fundamental change in the centralized system.

As a number of Soviet writers have pointed out,[3] no group in Soviet society stands only to gain from the economic and political reforms that Gorbachev is proposing. Survey results indicate, however, that the majority of the population feel that "they could work much more effectively under different economic conditions" (Zaslavskaia 1986, p. 1).[4] The real dilemma seems to be that there is no constituency strongly backing the reforms. While consumers, for example, may gain, they do not represent a group Gorbachev can turn to for support, because they are neither organized nor mobilized. Thus resistance is likely to persist.

In the past, political and social conservatism in the USSR effectively inhibited economic reform. For a variety of political and social reasons, leaders viewed the possible consequences of radical changes in the Soviet economic system (inflation or unemployment, for example) as undesirable. Concern over undesirable consequences was compounded by the experience of past reform efforts, which often had inconsistent goals and were implemented on a piecemeal basis at best. Certainly a common characteristic of Gorbachev's proposals is their ambiguity, stemming no doubt from a compromise between reform-oriented and conservative forces.

It is not unreasonable to ask why economic reforms stay on the leadership's agenda, especially if, as Gertrude Schroeder (1986) contends, they tend to exacerbate rather than solve the problem. Several possible explanations arise. Persistent shortages, especially of consumer goods, attract the attention of leaders, keeping the inadequacies of the centralized system in the limelight. Numerous accounts in the Soviet press suggest that leaders view the technological level of Soviet industry as unsatisfactory, and feel an urgency to improve the situation. Finally, one may view reform proposals as an indication of the direction Soviet leaders favor for the economic system.

The essays collected here provide snapshots, from a variety of perspectives, of the Soviet economic bureaucracy on the "treadmill" of reform. Schroeder, Leggett, and Kushnirsky compare Gorbachev's proposals to past Soviet reform efforts and to reforms implemented in other countries. Theen and Dyker analyze the impact of reforms on different sectors of the Soviet economy (agriculture, investment). Toumanoff and Linz examine how past reforms have been viewed from the top and bottom of the economic bureaucracy, by planners and managers.

In the time since these papers were written, Gorbachev has made a number of dramatic economic and political reform proposals. At the plenary meeting of the Central Committee in June 1987, Gorbachev outlined features of what Joseph Berliner (1987) views as a New Economic System. In the heavily guided, semi-market system Gorbachev proposed, output would no longer be determined by a detailed national plan. Instead, enterprises would decide what to produce on the basis of orders solicited from other enterprises. To obtain materials for production, enterprises would no longer submit requisitions to planning authorities (who in turn specify suppliers and authorize amounts). Instead, enterprises would find and place orders with their own suppliers (either producing enterprises or wholesale outlets). The state would continue to price basic commodities, but all other prices would be determined by negotiation between buyers and sellers. Producers would be expected to compete for sales and use net profits to increase the incomes of workers and management. Permanent subsidies to enterprises would be phased out, and unprofitable firms would face reorganization or dissolution. In this new economic system, Gosplan would continue to draw up national plans that identify the main directions of economic activity, the rate and structure of investment, and the regional distribution of economic activity. National plans would serve primarily to guide ministries and enterprises by taxes, subsidies, access to bank credit, and setting norms for evaluating enterprise activity.

Under the proposed system, party officials would no longer have the responsibility for monitoring enterprise operations and performance. Moreover, the consolidation of ministries, and corresponding reductions in staff, would lessen ministry power over enterprises. Enterprise managers would necessarily face more competition and greater risk. And workers, to the extent that wages would be determined by productivity or product quality, would no longer be guaranteed a job or stable income.

There is a great deal at stake. Much has been promised; and while much has been given, it is not as much as was promised. The reforms that Gorbachev has proposed, quite independent of the political and social changes that may occur, have the potential for immeasurably improving the daily lives of the Soviet people. They hold out the possibility of an end to endless queues and the mutually demeaning institutions of bribery and the second economy. And they open the prospect of a new relationship of the Soviet Union to the rest of the world, with respect to science, technology, diplomacy, and the ultimate issue of world peace. It is for this reason that not only the Soviet people, but the whole world is watching!

Notes

1. "The main precept of any bureaucracy is the maintenance of the status quo. The most important thing is not to change anything" (V. Bykov, *Literaturnaia gazeta*, no. 1 [1986]: 6).

2. Resistance to Gorbachev's proposed social and economic changes is analyzed by Anatolii Butenko in "Perestroika i sotsial'naia bor'ba v obshchestve," *Moscow News*, no. 1 (January 4, 1987). He categorizes popular response to Gorbachev's proposals by identifying four groups in Soviet society: those who wholeheartedly embrace "restructuring" (*perestroika*); those who understand the necessity of working in a new way, but don't know how to go about it in practice; those who prefer to wait and see (the skeptics and cynics); and those who actively oppose the reform proposals. Most notably, Tat'iana Zaslavskaia (1983, 1986) has pointed out the fact that while essential features of the Soviet system need fundamental change, vested interests within the system oppose reform and will do anything to prevent it.

3. See, for example, Zaslavskaia (1983, 1986), Butenko (1987), and Iakovlev (1987).

4. Vladimir Shlapentokh argues that the political thinking of Soviet leadership in many respects may be outstripping the capacity and the desire of society to assimilate these ideas ("Ideological Conflicts in the Period of Glasnost," unpublished paper, Michigan State University, October 1987). This may be why, for example, Iakovlev's speech (delivered April 17, 1987, to the Presidium of the USSR Academy of Sciences) which sets out Gorbachev's ideological platform was published in full in *Vestnik Akademii Nauk SSSR* (no. 6, June 1987: 51–80, circulation 5,000) but only in part in *Kommunist* (no. 8, 1987: 3–22, circulation 1 million).

References

Berliner, J., "Continuities in Management from Stalin to Gorbachev," in *Soviet Industry from Stalin to Gorbachev: Essays on Management and Innovation* (Edward Elgar Ltd. and Cornell University Press), forthcoming 1988.

Butenko, Anatolii, "Perestroika i sotsial'naia bor'ba v obshchestve," *Moscow News,* no. 1 (January 4, 1987).

Schroeder, Gertrude E., "Soviet Economic Reform Decrees: More Steps on the Treadmill," Joint Economic Committee, *Soviet Economy in the 1980s: Problems and Prospects* (Washington, D.C.: US GPO, 1982), pp. 65–88.

———. "Gorbachev: Radically Implementing Brezhnev's Reforms," *Soviet Economy* (October-December 1986), pp. 289–301.

Zaslavskaia, T., "Novosibirsk Report," *Survey* (December 1985).

———. *Sovetskaia Rossiia* (January 7, 1986), p. 1.

REORGANIZATION
AND REFORM
IN THE
SOVIET ECONOMY

Gertrude E. Schroeder

Organizations and Hierarchies
The Perennial Search for Solutions

Introduction

Throughout the six decades of centrally planned socialism, the Soviet leadership has displayed an abiding faith in the efficacy of changes in organizational forms and in the formal relationships among units in the hierarchies as solutions for perennial economic problems. As a consequence such changes have been numerous and frequent, but the problems have persisted. A vigorous new leader, Mikhail Gorbachev, is attacking them once more, calling for "radical economic reform" and a "restructuring" of society amounting to a "revolution."[1] As revealed in his actions during his first two years of tenure, Gorbachev, too, shares the faith of his predecessors in the efficacy of reorganizations of bureaucracies and redefinitions of "rights" among levels in the administrative hierarchy.

The purpose of this paper is to provide historical perspective for the current round of hierarchical reforms as they concern the economy, as well as to describe them in some detail and to assess their likely results. For analytical purposes, the term "hierarchical economic reforms" will be defined here as having three major aspects: the number and kind of formal organizations and their functions, a definition of the formal rights and obligations of the organizations in a line relationship to one another, and the set of incentives and controls established to ensure that those rights and responsibilities are carried out in the interest of state-set goals. This paper deals only with the first two aspects and focuses on the postwar period, leaving the complex third one for a future endeavor. Each section will first provide historical background and then describe

---

The author teaches at the University of Virginia.

the actions taken or *en train* under Gorbachev. The first section sketches changes in organizational forms *per se*, using as a framework the familiar staff-and-line classification. To delineate the problem of staff organization and functions, we limit ourselves to those concerned with planning, supply, price setting, and coordination of research and development. Similarly, with regard to the problem of organizing line functions, we deal primarily with the industrial sector of the economy. The second section treats the saga of changes in the formal relationships among major line organizations—ministries (or their equivalents)—and the business firms. It also deals briefly with the relationships between the center and the republics and local soviets. A final section provides a summary of Gorbachev's actions thus far and assesses their likely impact.

Changes in Forms of Organization
—Centralized Staff Functions

How best to organize the bureaucratic mechanism to replace free markets and administer state-owned property has proved to be an intractable problem. Four indispensable functions must be provided for: planning of production; allocation of material inputs and investment goods; price determination; and management of the research, development, and innovation process. The Soviet government has sought to direct these matters through central staff agencies, and each of these areas has been the scene of organizational ferment throughout the postwar period.

Planning

In 1946, a single organization—the State Planning Committee (Gosplan)—was in charge of all central planning. In June 1955, Gosplan was split, retaining the function of long-range planning, with short-term planning going to the new State Economic Commission. The latter was abolished in 1957 and its functions returned to Gosplan. In 1960, a State Economic Council charged with long-term planning was created, only to be abolished three years later. Gosplan now had all central planning functions, along with supply and pricing functions and jurisdiction over a number of sectoral state committees.[2] As a result of the 1965 reforms, Gosplan's supply and pricing functions were vested in new agencies, and the sectoral state committees were transformed into ministries, over which Gosplan did not have administrative authority. Its functions were codified in a formal statute issues in 1968. During the next 20 years, the burdens imposed on Gosplan steadily increased, as the complexity of central planning tasks multiplied along with the size of the economy and as a result of decisions to graft detailed planning for numerous "complexes" onto the established planning routine. With the establishment of interdepartmental commissions to oversee implementation of some of these complexes, Gosplan *de facto* also took on the status of a ministry, directly planning and allocating resource flows to the complexes.[3] In the process, Gosplan was reorganized internally and its powers codified in a new statute adopted in June 1982.[4]

Although Gorbachev has replaced several key personnel in Gosplan, among them its chairman and deputy chairman, he is clearly dissatisfied with the committee's present role. In his address to the 27th Party Congress, he spoke of the need to reorganize the work of Gosplan, so as to make it the "real scientific-economic headquarters of the country," freed from the need to deal with routine economic problems.[5] Precisely what this means for Gosplan's structure and functions is obscure, but revision of the committee's statute apparently is among several key pieces of legislation now being drafted.

Supply

As for planning, the search for the "perfect" organizational arrangement for carrying out centralized rationing of materials and equipment to producers has been continuous. In 1946, Gosplan had that function. In 1947, it was given to a newly created State Committee for Material-Technical Supply (Gossnab). Gossnab was abolished in 1953, along with a State Committee for Supply of Food and Consumer Goods that had been assigned part of Gossnab's turf in 1951. The entire function was then given to Gosplan, which kept it for two years, when it was transferred to the new State Economic Commission. With its abolition two years later, Gosplan regained the supply function at the center but shared part of it with the Regional Economic Councils (Sovnarkhozy). With the demise of the latter in 1965, the responsibility for administering the rationing system was vested in a recreated Gossnab, although Gosplan retained responsibility for the allocation of some 2,000 major products. A statute on Gossnab adopted in May 1969 spelled out the committee's functions.[6] In 1981, the distribution of petroleum prod-

ucts was removed from Gossnab and assigned to a new State Committee for the Supply of Petroleum Products.

Although its status has otherwise remained intact, Gossnab's performance has been the subject of constant criticism. The outlines are as yet
unclear, but Gorbachev has stated his perception that the hoary problem
must be tackled anew: "The system of material-technical supply is in
need of serious improvement."[7] As of now, Gossnab's organizational
status does not seem to be in jeopardy, for the list of draft legislation to
be adopted during 1986–90 calls for proposals that will produce "an
enhancement of the role and responsibility of USSR Gossnab and its
local authorities for the uninterrupted provision of the economy with
material resources and their efficient use."[8] Although there is much
talk about expanding "wholesale trade in the means of production,"
the actions taken thus far amount merely to some reduction in the
bureaucratic paperwork associated with materials rationing by allowing small-scale users to deal directly with regional Gossnab units.[9]

Price-setting

Before 1965, responsibility for setting and enforcing the prices of all
important products was scattered among many agencies—industrial
ministries, the Sovnarkhozy, the Ministries of Finance and of Trade,
the Committee for State Control. Coordination and control at the
national level was exercised by a Prices Commission of the USSR
Council of Ministers and a Bureau for Prices under Gosplan. In April
1965, the price-setting functions were assigned to a newly created
Committee for Prices under USSR Gosplan, with counterpart committees at republic and local levels. Several years later the committee was
removed from Gosplan and established as a union-republic State Committee for Prices under the USSR and Republic Councils of Ministers.[10] In addition to overseeing periodic major revisions of centrally
set prices, the committee issues the rules for decentralized setting of
prices, approves such prices, proposes policy changes, and is in charge
of the enforcement of all state prices and pricing regulations.

As part of his reform program, Gorbachev has called for more
"flexible" prices to influence economic behavior of both firms and the
public. There has been little action as yet, but the government has
mandated the drafting of legislative proposals for the "plan-oriented
reorganization of the pricing system." The State Pricing Committee is
one of the designated drafters.[11]

Research and Development and the Introduction of New Technology

For decades, the government has believed it necessary to have a distinct organization charged with overseeing the process of scientific-technical research and ensuring the introduction of the results into production. A State Committee for New Technology (Gostekhnika) was established in December 1947 and charged with "the forced introduction of new technology into the economy." It was abolished in 1951, only to be revived four years later and given the primary task of its predecessor, along with the job of coordinating all research and development (R and D). In 1957 it became the State Scientific-Technical Committee and in 1961 was transformed into a State Committee for Coordination of Scientific Research, with considerably broader authority over the content and conduct of the R and D process. In 1965 this committee was reconstituted as a revived Gostekhnika and charged, among other things, with developing a "unified national policy for science and technology" and making long-range forecasts of specific scientific and technological developments as inputs into long-range planning. Although Gostekhnika has remained organizationally intact since 1965, its work has come under fire from Gorbachev, who has criticized it for failing to restructure its work rapidly enough.[12] What such restructuring entails may be revealed in a set of regulations now being drafted to govern the committee's work. In the meantime, a new body dealing with science policy and implementation in one major area has been created—the State Committee for Computers and Information Science, set up in March 1986.[13]

Changes in Organizational Forms —Line Authority

In Soviet thinking, there are two basic ways to organize the production process—the "branch principle" and the "territorial principle." Each has its costs and benefits. In practice the Soviet government has had to combine them, conducting a perpetual search for the optimal combination. During the first few decades of central planning, the branch principle dominated. In the industrial sector, a rapidly increasing number of central ministries organized along product lines were charged with overseeing the production process. In 1957 Nikita Khrushchev engineered the replacement of the system of management through branch ministries with management through regional economic councils (Sovnarkhozy); the new scheme was intended to counter the inefficiencies created by overcentralization in decision-making, excess parochialism by ministries, and inattention to territorial planning. But that innovation proved politically and economically unviable, quickly creating more problems than it solved. Reorganizations of one kind or another were introduced as solutions.[14] The number of Sovnarkhozy was successively reduced, the few extant ministries were soon joined by two dozen or so state committees organized by major product groups as before, and coordinating bodies were piled one on top of another. The result was administrative chaos. After its architect's ouster in 1964, this ''hare-brained scheme'' was speedily terminated and the form of economic organization returned to the branch principle. We focus on the experience with branch ministries.

Administration of the industrial production process along product lines requires decisions on a number of key points: How many ministries should there be? Should they be answerable only to the central government (all-union ministries), to both the central and republic governments (union-republic ministries), or solely to republic authorities (republic ministries)? Which product groups require separate ministries? Since Soviet administrators have not been able to devise principles on the basis of which to answer such questions, administration via ministries has been a saga of perpetual improvisation. Thus, there were 33 industrial ministries in July 1946, 26 in February 1953, 12 as of March 15, 1953, and 25 as of April 26, 1954. On August 3, 1966, after the return of the ministerial form, there were 31—19 all-union ministries and 12 union-republic ministries. Thereafter, ministries proliferated; in early 1985, the number of industrial ministries stood at 47—27 of the all-union type and 22 of union-republic type.

During the first two years of his tenure, Gorbachev has displayed a conviction that there is much to gain from reorganization of the economic bureaucracy, along with wholesale replacement of bureaucrats. One all-union ministry—for nuclear power production—has been created, and three union-republic food-processing ministries have been abolished. Their functions were absorbed by a new State Committee for the Agro-Industrial Complex (Gosagroprom) created in November 1985; this Committee also took over the tasks of the abolished Ministries of Agriculture and Rural Construction and the State Committee for Supply of Equipment to Agriculture.[15] The concept of putting organizations managing related activities under a single roof, exemplified by Gosagroprom, was extended to the construction industry in September 1986.[16] That reorganization designated the State Committee for Construction as the czar of the country's "construction complex," managing four all-union ministries organized on a territorial basis, two organized on a type-of-project basis, and the Ministry of Construction Materials. Thus implementing the idea of "super-ministries" long advocated by Brezhnev, the Gorbachev administration also has established a Bureau for Machine-Building to coordinate the activities of the eleven civilian machinery production ministries, a Bureau for the Fuel-Energy Complex to oversee the six relevant production ministries, a Bureau for Social Development to oversee programs related to improving the population's welfare and development of social infrastructure, and a State Foreign Economic Commission to coordinate all such activities.[17] All of these agencies are permanent bodies under the USSR Council of Ministers, and each is chaired by a Deputy Chairman of the Council. Apparently there is a great deal of confusion over the precise function and authority of these new bodies and on how they relate to other relevant agencies. The situation is similar with regard to the State Committee for Computers and Information Sciences set up in March 1986.

Besides the problems associated with determining the number and jurisdiction of branch ministries in the industrial sector, Soviet authorities have perceived difficulties in how to manage the major sub-branches within a branch ministry. Under the ministerial system the traditional solution was to establish main administrations (*glavki*) for sub-groups of products. A major reform decree adopted in April 1973 called for the establishment of All-Union Industrial Associations (*ob"edineniia*) to serve as intermediate links between the ministries and newly created production associations or large enterprises.[18] These Industrial Associations could be organized either on the basis of the ministerial *glavki*, which they were supposed to replace, or along national lines encompassing all enterprises producing given products, a form that would involve transfers of jurisdiction over firms among the various ministries. The Associations also could be organized along regional lines. The Industrial Associations were supposed to operate on the principle of economic accountability (*khozraschet*) like their subordinate enterprises. Judging from a variety of anecdotal evidence, this reform never amounted to much, for the Industrial Associations failed to specialize as intended and behaved much like the former *glavki*. Premier Ryzhkov, in his speech to the Supreme Soviet in June 1986, stated that the Industrial Associations, "which have not proved their worth," had been abolished in the machinery ministries.[19] The Twelfth Five-Year Plan calls for the adoption throughout most of industry of a two-tier management structure consisting only of ministries and associations or enterprises. In the machinery industries, however, this move has entailed the resurrection of numerous *glavki* and placed severe burdens on the ministries.[20]

Another set of organizational decisions has centered around the form of organization of the so-called "basic link"—the business firm. Traditionally, it has been the enterprise (*predpriiatie*), which was a legally independent entity with its own bank account and operated on the basis of *khozraschet* (economic accountability). During the Sovnarkhoz period, the authorities began to lobby for the amalgamation of enterprises into larger entities, variously labeled trusts or firms. In early 1965 there were about 500 firms, mainly uniting plants producing similar products within a given region. In some cases, the individual enterprises became divisions of the firm; in others, the enterprises retained their independent status, with the firm performing certain overhead functions and dealing directly with superior bodies. Although the Kosygin reforms called for the further merging of enterprises into "associations," little was done about it. In 1970 there were only 608 associations, accounting for 6.2 percent of industrial employment.[21] After Brezhnev at the 24th Party Congress called for the association to become the "basic link" in the future, the Party tried to put some steam into the merger movement. The Party–Government decree of April 1973 launched a full-scale effort to set up associations throughout industry, a task that was supposed to be completed by 1980.[22] This decree also provided for the establishment of science–production associations, combining production facilities with research-and-design institutes formerly subordinated directly to the ministries. Both forms were supposed to yield economies of scale, save on administrative costs, and spur technological progress. Although evaluations of the formation and performance of both kinds of associations were mixed, Party pressure for their formation persisted and the merger movement proceeded. At the end of 1975 there were 2,314 associations (about 100 of them science-production types) accounting for 24.4 percent of industrial output and 28.8 percent of employment; corresponding figures for the end of 1980 were 4,083; 48.2 and 50.1.[23] Five years later there were 4,378 associations (about 250 science-production types) accounting for 50.3 percent of output and 52.7 percent of employment.[24] In that year some 21 percent of all independent industrial enterprises were units in these associations; the rest remained outside that structure. The Directives for the Twelfth Five-Year Plan provide for the further development of the two kinds of associations and for the creation of intersector associations where appropriate. In addition, production-marketing associations are to be set up for consumer goods produced in light industry.

Intra-Hierarchical Relationships

How to define the rights and responsibilities of the various levels in the line hierarchy of economic management has posed a dilemma from the outset of central planning—a dilemma that is often couched in terms of administrative centralization vs. decentralization. Since the center does not possess all available knowledge and cannot do everything, the essential problem is one of splitting up tasks and assigning responsibilities among levels in the hierarchy so as to get the job done in the most effective manner and to prevent anything important from being overlooked. [25] The vacillation over these matters over the years has involved two chains in the hierarchy: (1) the relationships between the ministries (or equivalents) and the producing units (enterprises or their equivalent) and (2) the relationships among the central government, the republic governments and the local soviets in economic matters. Gorbachev has already attacked the hoary problem with regard to both hierarchies.

Relationships between Ministries and Enterprises

Ministries have been charged with responsibility for development of the branch as a whole and for meeting the specific production targets set for it in annual and five-year plans. The relevant legal documents are supposed to accord them powers sufficient to meet those responsibilities. Each subordinate enterprise is responsible for carrying out its assigned share of the total ministerial task, and relevant documents are supposed to accord it the necessary powers (rights) to perform its task. The theory of economic accountability (*khozraschet*), in turn, implies that the enterprise is to have autonomy or freedom of action to carry out its assigned task as it sees fit within established parameters. To implement these concepts, the authorities in the postwar period have perceived a need not only to draft legal documents (statutes) spelling out the nature, rights, and responsibilities of the various levels in the hierarchy, but also to devolve more of both to the lowest level—the enterprise. The outcome has been an ebb and flow of decentralization and "creeping" or "galloping" recentralization. In August 1953, a decree enlarged the powers of ministries at the expense of Gosplan, and two years later enterprises were given a bit more authority vis-a-vis the ministries. During the Sovnarkhoz interregnum, the problem continued to fester, for it seems that the Sovnarkhozy were prone to exercise rigid control over the enterprises under their jurisdiction. A Party Plenum held in November 1962 advocated greater autonomy for firms and called for drafting a statute that would broaden their rights and also give the work collective a greater role in management. Such a statute was promulgated in October 1965 as part of the reform package,[26] and a similar document governing the ministries was adopted in July 1967.[27] Subsequently, similar statutes were promulgated for the three kinds of associations—industrial, production, and science-production.[28]

The statutes defining the competence of the enterprises (associations) and the ministries are couched in broad terms, so as to be of general applicability and utility as guides for behavior. Worthy of note is the fact that these statutes assign as a basic function to each level the fulfillment of its respective state plan. In the case of the ministry, that plan is approximately the sum of the plans of subordinate enterprises; the statute explicitly states that the minister himself "bears personal responsibility for the tasks and duties imposed on the ministry." The statutes were written to accord with the 1965 economic reform documents, which laid great stress on the theme of increasing the economic independence of enterprises. In implementing that general objective, these reforms used as instruments a reduction in the number of plan targets assigned to enterprises by superior agencies, explicit enlargement of enterprise decision-making authority over labor and investment, and a restructuring of the financial relationships between the firm and the state so as to permit the firm to finance from its own "earned" funds a larger share of its total planned expenditures, including investment. The following plan targets were to be set centrally: volume of sales, the basic product assortment in physical units, the wage fund, total profits and the profit rate relative to fixed and working capital, payments to and from the state budget, the volume of centralized investment and commissionings of new fixed assets, assignments for introduction of new technology, and allocations of materials and equipment. Over the following 20 years, in the course of reforming the 1965 reforms, the number of centrally set targets has increased, and changes have been made in the basic list in some cases.[29] In addition, complaints were perennial that the ministries added still other mandatory targets and changed them frequently. Moreover, the specific new freedoms of decision-making granted to firms in respect to determination of employment and bonuses and deciding small-scale investments were retracted, because the authorities did not like the decisions taken and because firms' efforts to acquire resources to carry out their proposed projects competed with the state's investment priorities. With regard to the other instrument—enterprise self-finance—nothing much happened after the initial extension of authority, and most industrial enterprises continued to receive some funding from the budget, despite a major economic reform decree of July 1979 that demanded action on the self-finance front.[30]

Faced with dramatically worsened economic performance, Brezhnev's immediate successor, Yuri Andropov, decided to try once more to attack the economy's intractable problems by expanding the scope of decision-making accorded to enterprises. A decree adopted in July 1983 authorized an experiment in selected enterprises of two all-union ministries and three republic consumer goods ministries.[31] Under this experiment, selected enterprises once again were given fewer centrally set plan targets, accorded the right to decide the nature of some investment and R and D projects financed from the firm's own funds, and allowed more freedom to decide matters concerning wages and bonuses. They were also placed on a system of partial self-finance. A Law on the Labor Collective, also adopted in July 1983, was an attempt to give enterprise workers more voice in enterprise decision-making, especially on matters relating to employee welfare.[32] Konstantin Chernenko's contribution was to authorize extension of Andropov's experiment to most other civilian industrial ministries as of January 1, 1985.

In many forums, Gorbachev has stated the belief that one of the keys to better economic performance lies in strengthening centralized planning and management while simultaneously substantially expanding the autonomy of the enterprise based on self-finance (*samofinansirovanie*), the principle of paying its own way (*samookupaemost'*), and self-management. These ideas are important planks in his program for restructuring society (*perestroika*) and radical economic reform (*radikal'naia ekonomicheskaia reforma*). He has moved vigorously to translate these ideas into actions, securing Politburo approval of a new Draft

Statute on the State Enterprise (Association),[33] a decree according firms more authority over administrative-management expenditures,[34] and decrees that extend the provisions of the so-called "experiment" launched by Andropov (or some variant thereof) to all of industry and several other sectors as of January 1, 1987.[35] At the same time, he has engaged in a ministry-bashing vendetta of unprecedented magnitude. During his first two years, he has replaced over three-fifths of the ministers and heads of state committees dealing with the economy. While holding them "personally responsible" for the shortcomings of their respective sectors, he excoriates them for foot-dragging, conservativism, exercising petty tutelage over subordinate enterprises in violation of their statutory rights, and resisting "restructuring," both of the ministry itself and of its subordinate enterprises.

In February 1987, the new Draft Statute on the State Enterprise was published, after having been remanded once by the Polituro for further work. This lengthy document has the flavor of having been drafted by a committee, being couched in rather loose language designed to accommodate diverse points of view. In essence, the new Draft Statute is a rewrite of the existing one to accommodate the specific features of the current round of economic reforms. Thus, it (1) applies to all state entities regardless of sector; (2) defines enterprise rights and responsibilities in terms of self-finance and paying its own way; (3) states that firms must conduct their operations in accord with "plan targets, state orders, and long-term normatives"; (4) states that the list of targets, resource allocations and normatives set centrally for firms in annual and five-year plans is to be determined by the Council of Ministers and forbids ministries from imposing others or changing the normatives; (5) permits the enterprise to sue its ministry if it incurs losses as a result of complying with an illegal ministry order; (6) amends the 1983 Law on the Labor Collective to provide for election of a permanent enterprise Council to monitor fulfillment of decisions taken at meetings of the collective and also for the election of enterprise directors and heads of lower-level divisions by secret or open vote of the enterprise work force; (7) specifically states that superior organs may close down enterprises that cannot pay their own way, in which case employees must be given two months' notice and may receive their wages for up to three months. A long list of articles in the statute spell out specific "rights" accorded to the firm, few of which are new. According to Gorbachev, the Statute on the State Enterprise will be supplemented by statutes defining the authority of the ministries and key state committees vis-a-vis the enterprise.[36]

As noted earlier, Soviet reformers have sought to devolve authority to firms by reducing the number of centrally set control figures specified in plans. As of January 1, 1987, all industrial enterprises are supposed to be operating under the rules of the Andropov-initiated "experiment," which, among many other things, purports once more to cut the number of centrally set plan targets. But at the same time it greatly expands the use of centrally-set normatives. According to the most complete list available, the following targets and limits are fixed for the firm in annual or five-year plans or both: growth of output, volume of sales taking into account contractual obligations, tasks for introducing new technology, output of basic products in physical units, with separate lines for new technology and items for export, share of goods in the highest quality category in total sales; growth of labor productivity, total profits, limits on material expenditures per ruble of output, limits on and commissionings from state centralized investment funds, limits for rationed material-technical inputs, assignments for reducing expenditures per ruble of output, export deliveries in convertible currencies, and wage fund for nonindustrial personnel.[37] The following norms are set: increase in wages per ruble of net output, wages of R and D personnel as a percentage of the volume of work, norms for deductions into the production-development fund (from profits and amortization), deductions from profits into the incentive and social-cultural development funds, and deductions from profits into the state budget and into various ministerial funds, such as the unified fund for financing R and D and introduction of new technology. Only slightly fewer targets, limits, and norms are fixed for firms in what is regarded as a more "progressive" version of the reforms also put into effect in January 1987 in five industrial ministries and a few other entities. These rules are patterned after those tried out in the much-touted experiments in the Sumy Machinery Science-Production Association and the Togliatti Automobile plant (AvtoVAZ).[38] Apparently the principal difference between this scheme and the one more generally applicable is a much simpler set of norms for allocating profits—fixed as specified shares of profits for each planned use. In addition to this basic list, we know that recent emendations establish norms that limit the size of administrative-management expenditures[39] and specify mandatory annual reductions in inventory-sales ratios.[40] There are probably other directive plan targets (e.g., for production of consumer goods and provision of consumer services), and other norms, such as that relating the permissible growth of wages to the increase in labor productivity.

A prominent feature of Gorbachev's reform program is the transfer of enterprises and ministries to a system of full financial autonomy, whereby they are to be required to finance all current and capital expenditures from their own revenues. Although self-finance was mandated by the July 1979 reform decree (and also was envisaged in the 1965 reform decree), it had been introduced in only a few ministries and a handful of enterprises. Now, Gorbachev is forcibly implementing that provision. In theory, implementation of the principles of self-finance and a related concept, "paying one's own way," along with fewer centrally set parameters, will make the enterprise and its collective fully autonomous, self-managed and independent of budget subsidies. The firm is supposed to be allowed to decide for itself how to spend the profits it has earned, after making obligatory payments of taxes and contributions to centralized ministerial funds. The firm's operations under self-finance, however, are regulated by numerous instructions issued by the Council of Ministers' Commission to Improve Planning, Management, and the Economic Mechanism, headed by Gosplan Chairman Nikolai Talyzin and charged with working out reform proposals and drafting appropriate legislation.[41] As before, the new rules require firms to establish three incentive funds (for bonuses, for social-cultural development, and for investment), fix separate norms, for transferring monies from profits and other sources into the three funds, and specify the uses to which the funds may be put.

In addition, the firm is now supposed to be allowed to retain all of its amortization charges that are deducted from costs to help finance investment. Only for new construction or in exceptional circumstances are budget funds to be granted for investment or any other purpose. If the firm fails to earn planned profits, the collective itself will suffer through reduced bonuses and curtailed opportunities for investment. Ministries are no longer supposed to be permitted to redistribute profits from one firm to another, as they did in the past. Nonetheless, because of the wide disparity in profitability rates among industrial enterprises (a consequence of Soviet price-setting on the basis of average costs) many enterprises either operate at planned losses or cannot earn sufficient profits to finance normal incentive funds and planned investment. Hence, enterprise-specific norms are still needed, as are various ministerial reserve funds and substantial budget grants. Along with all this, a centrally mandated reform of wage and salary scales and work norms is to be carried out within the framework of enterprise autonomy and self-finance, with each enterprise being required to use its own "earned" funds to cover any wage increases that may result from the new scales.[42] A forty-page set of "recommendations" has been issued by the authorities to "guide" firms in carrying out the reform, which is intended to widen earnings differentials and gear each worker's pay to his productivity.[43] Finally, the current round of reforms, like those of 1965, explicitly accords broader decision-making authority to enterprises in the fields of labor and investment. In the case of the latter, decisions must be incorporated in detail in annual plans, in order to obtain claims on the required resources, which continue to be centrally rationed.

Relations between the Center, the Republics, and the Local Soviets

The issues involved in the search for the optimal distribution of decision-making authority between the center and the periphery are similar to those surrounding center–ministry–firm relationships. The center cannot know and do everything and, particularly in a large, diverse geographic entity like the USSR, necessarily must delegate a measure of authority to administrative subdivisions. The perennial dilemma has been how to secure desired efficiency in administration without losing control. In the Soviet case, this familiar problem has an added politically sensitive dimension, because the USSR is constituted as a federation of nominally autonomous republics, each of which is the traditional homeland of a distinct ethnic group that in nearly all cases dominates its population. Stalin resolved the issue by maintaining tight central control over economic affairs via an ever-growing number of economic ministries centered in Moscow. The republic councils of ministers and their subordinate units were kept on a tight leash. They gained a considerable measure of authority during the short-lived Sovnarkhoz era, although to combat endemic manifestations of "localism" and predilections for regional autarky, several attempts were made to tighten central controls. With the restoration of the ministerial system in 1965, the authority of regional administrative bodies was sharply reduced. At that time, however, the national leadership indicated that the republics would be accorded more decision-making authority. Specifically, Premier Kosygin stated that republic Gosplans would be permitted to draw up regional development plans, including plans involving firms of all-union ministries located on their territory.[44] Four years later, Gosplan issued methodological instructions dealing with these matters.[45]

During the 1970s, there was much discussion about how best to combine regional and sectoral planning and about the respective roles of central and regional administrative bodies in the process. Although regional authorities continued to lobby for more elbow-room and more decision-making authority, the new 1977 Constitution essentially maintained the status quo. But the dilemma became more acute as the size and complexity of the economy continued to increase. The economic reform decree of July 1979 instructed the ministries to review their annual and five-year plans with the appropriate Republic Councils of Ministers, which, in turn, were directed to draw up and monitor the implementation of territorial plans for "production of local building materials and consumer goods" and for "construction of housing and municipal and cultural facilities."[46] A decree issued in early 1981 ostensibly extended the authority and responsibility of the local soviets by (1) requiring enterprises, before submitting their plans to their superior ministry, to send them for concurrence from the local soviets in regard to "land use, environmental protection, construction, labor utilization, and social-cultural measures"; (2) stipulating that plants producing primarily for local consumption should be put under the jurisdiction of the local soviet; and (3) "as an experiment," assigning to the republic Councils of Ministers all funds, including those of the ministries, designated for investment in housing and services.[47]

Following up on Gorbachev's statement at the 27th Party Congress that a new look should be taken at the problem of efficient center-territorial distribution of powers, the government issued a major decree in July 1986 spelling out a broad range of rights and responsibilities of all regional bodies, with stress on those assigned to the local soviets.[48] The decree is highly complex, and its import hard to assess. Many of its provisions appear to repeat those in the 1979 and 1981 decrees or others that are in force. In general, however, the new decree extends the powers and responsibility of regional bodies in managing local infrastructure and requires closer coordination of all development plans affecting a given territory. The decree spells out a variety of instruments and forms of organization that local soviets may use to meet their assigned tasks and also gives them monitoring authority to ensure that locally based enterprises cooperate and carry out their assigned responsibilities vis-a-vis the local population. Specifically, they may organize local "construction complexes" to accomplish and coordinate municipal development projects, such as housing, and organize fund-sharing arrangements with local enterprises and organizations to accomplish similar projects. Also, the decree provides for the allocation of specific profit shares, turnover taxes, and other revenues to local budgets to enable local bodies to accomplish their greater responsibilities. A major decree adopted in September 1986 reorganized the construction industry to provide for the transfer of all building organizations under union-republic construction ministries to the jurisdiction of the respective Republic Councils of Ministers.[49] Finally, a new law on private economic activity gives local authorities a major role in administering, regulating, and facilitating the private endeavors permitted by the decree.[50]

Summary and Conclusions

Following the well-trodden path of his predecessors, General Secretary Gorbachev has attacked the problems of the economy by reorganizing bureaucratic structures and rearranging rights and responsibilities among the various layers in the administrative hierarchy. In the first two years of his tenure, here is what he has done: He has proposed altering the internal organizational structures of Gosplan and Gossnab; created one new state committee; abolished five ministries and created one new one; established coordinating bodies for the agro-industrial complex, for construction, for machinery production, for energy production, for foreign economic relations, and for social development; sanctioned the setting up of interbranch science-technology complexes and the abolition of the all-union industrial associations within the ministerial structure; revived the cooperative form of organizing economic activity in industry and the services; promulgated a new statute on the state enterprise and set in motion the drafting of similar statutes for key staff state committees and the ministries; introduced in industry and several other sectors new working arrangements that once again seek to cut the number of centrally set targets and parameters, grant more decision-making authority to firms with regard to managing labor and investment, and require firms to pay their own way financially; and adopted decrees that expand the decision-making authority and responsibilities of regional and local administrative units. He has also done many other things in areas that lie outside the scope of this paper.

Several decades ago, the Austrian economist Ludwig von Mises wrote: ''The problems of socialization cannot be solved by civil service instructions and reforms of organization."[51] For many decades, also, the governmental authorities in the Soviet Union, in effect, have been seeking to prove Mises wrong. They have yet to do so. Judging by his words as well as his actions thus far, Mikhail Gorbachev shares the belief of his predecessors that out there somewhere is the perfect organizational structure and the perfect set of instructions governing inter-hierarchical relationships that will make economic problems go away. As of this writing, the assorted reshufflings of organizational forms are still in the shake-down phase, but one may be skeptical of their yielding much benefit. They are a curious mixture of increased administrative centralization (the super-ministries) and administrative decentralization (more autonomy for firms and regional authorities). Although still rather amorphous, the new bundle of working arrangements does seem to sanction a considerably wider range of choice at lower levels in the hierarchy, thus increasing the flexibility of the system. At the same time, however, the cost of such greater flexibility seems to be the proliferation of monitors, each of which has been duly charged with the responsibility of ensuring that a given task is accomplished. Included among the ubiquitous monitors are the various levels of the Communist Party. The victim of this monitoring overkill is likely to be the beleaguered producing enterprise, whose efficiency can hardly be enhanced thereby.

As a result of Gorbachev's extension of the so-called "experiment" initiated by Andropov, all industrial enterprises and many of those in other sectors are supposed to be operating under one or another form of self-finance and "paying their own way." Soviet politicians, planners, and economists alike seem convinced that these new accounting and financial arrangements will, at long last, force the business firm to be efficient in all its activities, since it seemingly will both reap the rewards for success and bear the penalties for failure. Moreover, they seem to believe that, because it can now decide a wider range of matters for itself, the socialist firm will become more innovative and less risk-averse. Spurred by these new financial arrangements and added autonomy, and goaded by the requirement to operate on the basis of contracts with suppliers and customers, the firm will presumably strive to cut costs, welcome new technology, and be oriented toward pleasing customers with high-quality goods and machines of modern design. In a word, it will behave like a private enterprise in a market economy. But the politicians, planners, and economists are likely to be deeply disappointed. The new accounting arrangements are just that: they do not create markets or competition, and profit-based incentives will continue to be deprived of real economic (economizing) content, because administratively determined prices are retained. Moreover, despite the alleged greater autonomy, the firm's activities remain tightly constrained by centrally set plan targets and norms that fix all important variables. As of this writing, central planning has indeed been "strengthened," as intended, but the greater autonomy accorded to the producing units amounts to much ado about very little. Inauguration of truly radical hierarchical reforms, should they eventuate, will require a reassessment. Those in place as of now are puny.

Notes

1. *Pravda*, August 2, 1986.

2. The many changes made before 1965 are well described in Eugene Zaleski, *Stalinist Planning for Economic Growth, 1933-1952*, Chapel Hill, University of North Carolina Press, 1980, pp. 706–712; and Eugene Zaleski, *Planning Reforms in the Soviet Union, 1952-1966*, Chapel Hill, University of North Carolina Press, 1967, pp. 11–47.

3. These changes are described in Gertrude E. Schroeder, "Soviet Economic 'Reform' Decrees: More Steps on the Treadmill," in Joint Economic Committee, *Soviet Economy in the 1980s: Problems and Prospects*, Vol. 1, 1982, pp. 79–84.

4. *Sobranie postanovlenii pravitel'stva SSSR*, no. 20, 1982, pp. 372–383.

5. *Pravda*, February 26, 1986.

6. *Khoziaistvennaia reforma v SSSR*, Moscow, 1969, pp. 186–192.

7. *Pravda*, February 26, 1986.

8. *Vedomosti Verkhovnogo Soveta SSSR*, no. 37, September 10, 1986.

9. *Ekonomicheskaia gazeta*, No. 18, April 1986, p. 23. *Sobranie postanovlenii pravitel'stva SSSR*, no. 25, 1986, pp. 305–308.

10. For a full account see Morris Bornstein, "The Administration of the Soviet Price System," *Soviet Studies*, vol. 30, no. 4 (October 1978), pp. 466–490.

11. *Vedomosti Verkhovnogo Soveta SSSR*, no. 37, September 10, 1986.

12. *Pravda*, February 26, 1986.

13. *Pravda*, April 8, 1986.

14. See Zaleski, *Planning Reforms*, pp. 11–47.

15. *Pravda*, November 23, 1985.

16. *Pravda*, September 13, 1986.

17. *Izvestiia*, November 2, 1986.

18. *Pravda*, April 3, 1973.

19. *Pravda*, June 19, 1986.

20. *Khoziaistvo i pravo*, no. 2, 1987, pp. 54–58.

21. *Narodnoe khoziaistvo SSSR*, 1980, p. 121.

22. For a more complete discussion see Alice C. Gorlin, "The Soviet Economic Association," *Soviet Studies*, vol. 25, no. 1 (January 1974), pp. 3–27.

23. *Narodnoe khoziaistvo SSSR* 1980, p. 121.

24. *Narodnoe khoziaistvo SSSR* 1985, p. 91.

25. These conceptual matters, as well as the saga of Soviet efforts to deal with them, are described in Rush V. Greenslade and Gertrude E. Schroeder, "The Bureaucratic Economy," *Soviet Union/Union Sovietique*, 4, no. 2 (1977), pp. 314–329.

26. *Ekonomicheskaia gazeta*, no. 42, October 1965, pp. 25–29.

27. *Ekonomicheskaia gazeta*, no. 34, August 1967, pp. 7–9.

28. *Sovershenstvovanie khoziaistvennogo mekhanizma*, Moscow, 1980, pp. 224–277.

29. For a more detailed discussion of the reforms of the 1965 reforms see Gertrude E. Schroeder, "Soviet Economy on a Treadmill of 'Reforms,'" in Joint Economic Committee, *Soviet Economy in a Time of Change*, 1979, vol. 1, pp. 312–340.

30. *Pravda*, July 29, 1979.

31. *Pravda*, July 26, 1983.

32. *Pravda*, June 19, 1983.

33. *Pravda*, February 8, 1987.

34. *Sobranie postanovlenii pravitel'stva SSSR*, no. 23, 1986, pp. 397–399.

35. *Ekonomicheskaia gazeta*, no. 35, August 1985, pp. 11–14. *Ekonomicheskaia gazeta*, no. 47, November 1986, p. 17. *Pravda*, August 5, 1986.

36. *Pravda*, August 2, 1986.

37. *Mashinostroitel'*, no. 11, 1986, pp. 4–5.

38. *Ekonomicheskaia gazeta*, no. 47, November 1986, pp. 17–18.

39. *Sobranie postanovlenii pravitel'stva SSSR*, no. 23, 1986, pp. 397–99.

40. *Izvestiia*, December 15, 1986.

41. There are dozens of these issuances. See, for example: *Ekonomicheskaia gazeta*, no. 47, November 1986, p. 15; no. 49, December 1986, p. 17; no. 51, December 1986, p. 17; no. 52, December 1986, p. 14.

42. *Sobranie postanovlenii pravitel'stva SSSR*, no. 34, 1986, pp. 603–622.

43. *Sotsialisticheskii trud*, no. 2, 1987, pp. 57–96.

44. *Pravda*, September 28, 1965.

45. USSR Gosplan, *Metodicheskie ukazaniia k sostavleniiu gosudarstvennogo plana razvitiia narodnogo khoziaistva SSSR*, Moscow, 1969, pp. 672–683.

46. *Pravda*, July 29, 1979.

47. *Izvestiia*, March 29, 1981.

48. *Pravda*, July 30, 1986.

49. *Pravda*, September 13, 1986.

50. *Pravda*, November 21, 1986.

51. Ludwig von Mises, *Nation, State and Economy*, New York, New York University Press, 1983, pp. 194–195.

Robert E. Leggett

Gorbachev's Reform Program
"Radical" or More of the Same?

Background

In March 1985 Mikhail Gorbachev took charge of the latently powerful but troubled Soviet economy. Growth has been trending downward for several decades as the economy experienced repeated harvest failures, bottlenecks in industry, shortages of energy and labor, and chronically low productivity. GNP growth during the 11th Five-Year Plan (1981–85) had its worst showing of any five-year period since World War II (see Figure 1). Soviet planners are, in fact, searching for solutions to a number of serious problems that persist throughout the economy.

• Civilian industrial facilities are, to a large extent, old and technologically obsolete. The hi-tech revolution that has been transforming most Western economies since the 1970s has been less evident in the Soviet Union, resulting in a widening of the technology gap between the USSR and the West.

• Maintaining oil production—the USSR's major fuel—has been extremely costly, drawing heavily on Moscow's investment resources. At the same time, the drop in oil prices on world markets has markedly reduced hard-currency earnings from energy exports, thereby limiting Moscow's ability to buy needed machinery, food, and raw materials on Western markets.

• The farm sector continues to consume a disproportionate share of the USSR's labor, investment, and hard-currency resources, and to require growing subsidies to maintain stable retail food prices. Soviet farms manage to waste, by Moscow's own admission, 20 to 25 percent

The author is affiliated with the Central Intelligence Agency.

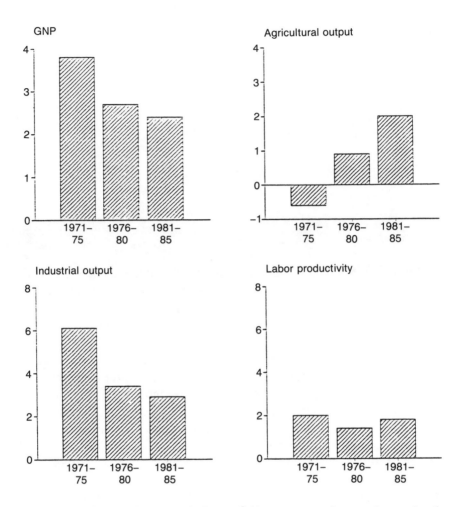

Figure 1 **USSR: Key Economic Indicators[a] (Average annual percentage rate of growth)**

[a]Unpublished Central Intelligence data; calculated at factor cost in 1982 rubles.

of their harvest annually.

• The quality of construction in the USSR is, by world standards, poor. The time taken to build new plants is so long, for instance, that the technologies incorporated in new facilities are often obsolete before they can be brought on line.

• Strict government control over foreign trade has reduced the potential effectiveness of imported technology and equipment. More generally, Moscow's long-standing inability to assimilate and diffuse imports in the civilian sector has greatly reduced the payoff to the economy from Western imports.

• The system of planning and management is too centralized and clumsy to manage effectively the increasingly complex and sophisticated economy. In addition, the perverse nature of the system of incentives discourages innovation and the efficient use of resources.

Meanwhile, improvements in living standards have tapered off as a result of the worsening performance of the economy, and popular discontent has grown. The latter has manifested itself in declining worker morale, more materialistic attitudes, an increase in "deviant" and "delinquent" behavior by Soviet youth, rising crime rates, alcohol and drug abuse, and a rising anti-Russian nationalism among ethnic groups. Leadership ineptitude and bureaucratic corruption, moreover, have compounded these problems.

Soviet regimes have not wavered, however, in their commitment to military power. Indeed, Moscow has used its military might to become a major player in world politics, but the cost has been high. The military build-up has been achieved through a commitment of the nation's best resources over the past two decades, resources that could have been used to modernize and expand the civilian economy. During the past ten years, for example, defense accounted for about 15 percent of Soviet gross national product each year—over twice as much as in the United States.

In sum, the most serious challenge facing the new regime is the state of the Soviet economy. The growth formula that had after the war propelled the USSR to the status of a world power—a massive infusion of labor and capital resources—no longer is workable. The highly centralized Soviet system of planning and management, in fact, appears to have been overwhelmed by the increasing size and complexity of the economy.[1]

Gorbachev's Strategy

General Secretary Gorbachev has moved very rapidly to put his stamp on economic policy. His immediate focus on key problems and the speed with which he has implemented his policies have been striking. The absence of delay suggests that at least the outlines of a game plan had been worked out before Gorbachev's advancement.

Gorbachev's goals for the future growth of the Soviet economy are laid out in the 1986–90 Plan and the Plan to the Year 2000.[2] The overall objective of these plans is a sharp acceleration in economic growth. A 4 percent per year rate of GNP growth is called for in the second half of the 1980s.[3] The long-term vision is even more ambitious, although few details are provided on the program's implementation. Economic growth is to accelerate to more than 5 percent a year during the 1990s.

New and Better Economic Policies

The leadership is pursuing a two-tiered strategy to turn the economy around, defined by near-term reliance on "human factors" and longer-term dependence on modernizing and restructuring the economy. "Human factors" include measures intended to instill more initiative in workers and managers, purge economic life of negative influences—corruption, drunkenness, and illegal economic activity—and enforce greater discipline in the work force. After the productivity increases associated with "human factor" gains runs its course, the leadership is counting primarily on continuing growth in efficiency spurred by improvements in planning and organization and, most especially, by the modernization of industry and the economy generally.

"Human Factor" Gains. The success of Gorbachev's program will depend in large part on the performance of the Soviet work force. In an attempt to exploit what the General Secretary refers to as the "human factor," a combination of measures are being utilized to strengthen discipline, improve workers' habits and attitudes, and weed out incompetents.

• The regime has promised more differentiation of wages based on the difficulty and skill requirements of jobs, a closer correlation between earnings and performance, and higher pay rates, matched by the increased availability of high-quality consumer durables, services, and food.[4]
• The labor discipline campaign that Yuri Andropov initiated, but which foundered somewhat under Konstantin Chernenko, has been revived.[5]
• A vigorous anti-alcohol campaign has been instituted. It serves as a daily reminder of the new leadership's seriousness and intensity in attacking social and economic problems.[6]

Workers at all levels, meanwhile, are being told that they could lose their jobs if they don't perform. The regime, in fact, is openly discussing allowing enterprises to cut the size of their work force. A recent edition of the Soviet magazine *Sovetskaia kul'tura,* for example, forecasts extensive layoffs in Soviet industry during the next 15 years and recommends that enterprises no longer be required to find jobs for dismissed workers.

Modernizing the Economy's Plant and Equipment. Gorbachev's game plan is to undertake a major overhaul of the economy. Reminiscent of Peter the Great's efforts to bring Russia, kicking and screaming if necessary, into the modern world, Gorbachev's goal is to raise the technological level in the USSR to that of the leading Western economies by the end of the century. The cornerstone of his plan is a major retooling and refurbishing of Moscow's production base.

• A greater quantity of investment goods (machinery, equipment and production facilities) is to be produced during 1986–90.[7]

• The quality of investment goods is to be raised. Old equipment, for example, is being retired more rapidly,[8] and quality standards of new equipment are being monitored more closely.[9] In addition, the construction sector has been reorganized to try and reduce the time required to build and renovate production facilities and to raise the quality of construction work.

• Measures are being taken to "administer" a higher rate of technological progress. The Academy of Sciences, for instance, has been directed to establish new departments oriented toward applied research, and interbranch scientific-technical complexes (MNTKs) have been established with a similar purpose.

The regime also has changed the structure and the distribution of investment expenditures. New construction, for example, is being curtailed. Instead, existing manufacturing facilities are being renovated and remodeled; equipment currently in use is being replaced as rapidly as possible with new machinery, as a way of quickly infusing more technology into the economy. At the same time, capital investment is being skewed more heavily toward the industries that produce machinery and equipment. Investment allocations during 1986–90 are to favor, in particular, high technology sectors such as machine tools, computers, and electronics (see Table 1).[10]

A Reform Program

Since taking power two years ago, Gorbachev has encouraged a freer and more open discussion of measures to change the economic system.

Table 1

USSR: Distribution of Investment in the 12th Five-Year Plan

| Sector | Billions of Rubles—1984 Prices | | Percentage Increase Plan 1986–90 over 1981–85 |
	1981–85 (Actual)	1986–90 (Plan)	
Total	843.2	1042	23.6
Productive	614.8	769	25
Industry	300.7	NA	NA
Fuels & power	108.4	147	35
Chemicals	22.6	34	50
Machine-bldg. & metal-working	73	100	37
Agriculture	156.2	165–170	about 7
Agro-industrial complex	269	343	28
Transportation	64.5	67	4.3
Railroads	24.1	25	4
Communications	5	7	40
Nonproductive	228.4	273	20

Source: Robert E. Leggett, ''Moscow's Investment Policy: The Key to Gorbachev's Program for Revitalizing the Soviet Economy,'' Joint Economic Committee, US Congress, forthcoming.

The central clearing house for new initiatives is a commission appointed by Gorbachev to manage the ''reform'' process centrally.*[11] This commission is chaired by First Deputy Chairman of the Council of Ministers and Gosplan head N.V. Talyzin; included in its membership are the Minister of Finance, the heads of the State Committees for Labor, Prices, and Material Supply (Gossnab), and ministers involved in industrial experiments. Soviet officials have indicated that the ''first phase'' of the reform process will be completed during the 12th Five-Year Plan. According to the Kremlin, the ultimate effect of the new measures will not be felt until the 1990s.

Better Planning and Management. Gorbachev has singled out the vast ministerial bureaucracy—with its organization along narrow departmental lines and its addiction to detailed management of the economy—as a road block to his program. He is taking measures to improve

*For purposes of analysis the definition of reform used in this paper is the one used by Janos Kornai in a recent article on the Hungarian economy. According to Kornai, reform is change in a socialist economic system that diminishes the role of bureaucratic coordination and increases the role of the market. See note 11.

interagency coordination—new superagencies have been created in agriculture, machine building, energy, construction, and foreign trade—to trim the central bureaucracy, and to increase the rights and responsibilities of individual enterprises. His aim is to achieve more effective central control over the main direction of the economy while leaving day-to-day management to lower levels.

Key performers in Gorbachev's new organization will be his frontline unit commanders—the industrial enterprise managers. The General Secretary needs a cadre of managers who can work far more independently than in the past—that is, a cadre of professionals who can solve problems on the spot without looking to Moscow for assistance, who are willing to take risks to improve plant performance, and who seek out innovative ideas and new technology—if he is to transform the economy from one that is tightly controlled by bureaucrats in Moscow into one that is more "self-regulating" and efficient.

Enterprise Autonomy in Industry. The leadership has adopted a three-stage agenda to curtail the administrative power of ministries over enterprises. The first stage began in 1984 when Andropov launched the five-ministry industrial experiment. Under the experiment, the number of enterprise performance indicators was reduced, the satisfaction of customers' demands for new and better products was made the major measure of enterprise success, and the firm's manager was given greater control over enterprise profits. According to Abel Aganbegian, one of Gorbachev's top economic advisors, all Soviet enterprises were to be operating under the regulations of the experiment as of January 1, 1987.

A second stage of restructuring began this year with the changeover of five industrial ministries, the Ministry of the Maritime Fleet, and the trade sector to "self-financing." Enterprises involved will be required to cover their costs and earn a profit. Soviet leaders have hailed this form of enterprise management as "the model of the future." An experiment commissioned in 1985 at two Soviet firms is serving as the prototype for this new form of enterprise management.[12]

The third part of the program is designed to make plants truly independent units by changing the finance, credit, and price systems. Wholesale trade is to be conducted between plants on the basis of contracts, and the number of central-plan indicators is to be reduced. Those that remain will be based on five-year plans. Ministry-enterprise relations will be on a contractual basis. To ensure that ministries do not interfere with an enterprise's autonomy, a law spelling out enterprise rights and duties was recently promulgated.[13]

Wage Reform. The Soviets claim to be instituting a more rational system of wages by establishing a tighter link between a worker's performance and his income. Few details have been published but apparently wages, on average, are to increase by 20–25 percent. The highest increases are earmarked for those professions important to Gorbachev's modernization program—designers, technologists and engineers. The difference between basic wage rates is also being widened—a sharp reversal from previous policies. Under Gorbachev's predecessors, a substantial reduction in pay differentials took place.

A major program in wage reform was commissioned in July 1985 on the Belorussian railroad. Under this experiment, the work force was markedly reduced and the salaries of those let go were used to raise the wages of the remaining employees on the basis of performance. According to Soviet data, the experiment has been a glowing success: wages have risen 23 percent since 1983 while labor productivity has increased 32 percent. Ten of the USSR's railroad networks apparently copied the system last year; Moscow claims that all the Soviet Union's railroads will follow suit by 1989.

Wholesale Trade. The distribution of manufactured goods and commodities in the USSR is done centrally under the direction of the State Committee for Material and Technical Supply (Gossnab) and the State Planning Committee (Gosplan). The supply system is one of the most intractable areas of the Soviet economy and is a major obstacle to improved economic performance. Suppliers are in a monopoly position vis-a-vis enterprises, often forcing them to accept inputs of inferior quality at inflated prices. Moreover, the unreliability of the system often forces enterprise managers to engage in inefficient and wasteful activities—such as the hoarding of resources and the in-house production of inputs.

At the 27th CPSU Congress, Gorbachev stated that "the system of material and technical supply is in need of serious improvement." A decree subsequently published calls for a number of ministries to convert to a system of wholesale trade on January 1, 1987.[14] But the decree is extremely vague and does not provide for an uncontrolled exchange of supplies between enterprises.

Also in the works is an effort to expand the role of consumer cooperatives in the trade network. State and collective farms have been authorized to sell up to 30 percent of their planned production quota of perishable produce—such as fruits and vegetables—through consumer cooperatives rather than state procurement channels.[15] In addition, any production in excess of annual procurement quotas can be sold through the consumer cooperative network, on the collective farm market, or to state agencies.[16]

Private Activity. The approval of a series of legislative initiatives since the 27th Party Congress last March indicates that the Gorbachev regime is embarking, albeit cautiously, on an expansion of opportunities for individual and small-group businesses in the USSR.

• A law on self employment, approved by the Supreme Soviet last November, sanctions a range of private activity from handicrafts to medical service.

• Decrees approved this past February permit groups of three or more people to form profit-sharing cooperatives to engage in three types of businesses: consumer services, food service, or production of consumer goods. This is a follow-on to regulations issued in October 1986 that permitted the formation of cooperatives to recycle raw materials or produce consumer goods from scrap.

• Regulations issued on May 15, 1986 explicitly sanction the formation of itinerant brigades of workers who hire themselves out to farms to perform construction or field work.[17]

New legislation sanctioning so-called individual labor activity could be the most significant, and the most controversial, changes made by the regime so far. Proponents of the legislation are hoping that it will quickly expand the range and improve the quality of goods and services available to the consumer—from taxis to medical care to auto repair. But the law permits little that has not already been legally permissible. Moreover, uncertainty over what prices can be charged, about tax rates, and the strict penalties for violations are not likely to lead to a large increase in private activity at any time soon. Moreover, the decree on "unearned income" passed last July has, at least for now, created an inhospitable climate in the USSR for private enterprise.

Foreign Trade. Some major changes have been made in the area of foreign trade which seem to portend a willingness on the Kremlin's part to expand its participation in the international trade arena. Most noteworthy are changes in the foreign trade apparatus and provisions for joint ventures.

• Reorganizing Trade. In September 1985, the Soviets announced an overhaul of the Ministry of Foreign Trade (MFT). As of January 1, 1987, more than 20 ministries and 70 large associations and enterprises were granted authority to conduct trade directly with foreign firms. Included in the list of Ministries are the State Agroindustrial Committee (Gosagroprom), the State Committee for Supplies (Gossnab), the Ministry of the Chemical Industry, and several machine-building ministries. The Soviets have indicated that, at least for the present, the MFT will continue to control trade in raw materials, food, and about 60 percent of machinery imports. As part of the reorganization the Soviets have created a coordinating commission made up of the heads of the major ministries and departments engaged in trade activities.

These changes should improve procedures for conducting trade in the USSR. They do nothing, however, to remedy the structural flaws that underlie the poor position of Soviet manufactured goods in world markets.

• Joint Ventures. The Soviets have passed a decree permitting joint ventures with Western firms. The decree allows up to 49 percent foreign equity, some foreign management of enterprises, the repatriation of profits, and other prerequisites to make such ventures attractive to Western firms. While most details remain vague, the general guidelines stipulate that the Western firm will furnish equipment, technology, and financing; the USSR will be responsible for providing the necessary "social infrastructure." The joint enterprise will be managed by a board on which Soviets occupy the positions of both chairman and director-general. Operationally, central planners will have no authority to impose production goals on these enterprises. Purchases from, and sales to, domestic enterprises are to be handled through foreign trade organizations, thus segregating these firms from the rest of the domestic economy.

The impact of joint ventures on the Soviet economy is likely to be minimal in the foreseeable future. Most Western firms will approach negotiations with the Soviets cautiously, especially since the regulations on forthcoming joint ventures are so vague and ill-defined. Moreover, having to deal with the cumbersome Soviet bureaucracy and the Soviet history of shoddy production will make businessmen wary of engaging in such ventures.

Assessing the Reform So Far

Mikhail Gorbachev, speaking before the 27th CPSU Congress in February 1986, boldly announced plans for a "radical reform" of the economic mechanism in the Soviet Union. Premier Ryzhkov repeated the General Secretary's call in his own address at the Party Congress and calls for "radical reform" have appeared with increasing frequency in the Soviet press since that time. Indeed, the changes being discussed have been billed by the leadership as some of the most significant in Soviet history, ranking alongside Lenin's New Economic Policy (NEP) in the early 1920s, Stalin's introduction of central planning in the late 1920s, and the Kosygin reforms of 1965.

Gorbachev appears to represent the emergence of a new breed of Soviet leader. He has, for example, shown little reluctance to break with the past. In a marked divergence from Moscow's previous reluctance to criticize Leonid Brezhnev by name, *Pravda* marked the 80th anniversary of his birth with a sweeping indictment of his last years in power.[18] Focusing on the key areas that Gorbachev has identified as demanding remedy, *Pravda* linked the problems of economic stagnation and political and moral decay directly to the late Soviet leader. The explicit attack on Brezhnev is a clear attempt by Gorbachev to justify his demands for change and for bolder measures to remedy the ills of the economy.

He has replaced many of the old guard who could be expected to resist change. The biggest upheaval in Soviet economic sciences in decades, for instance, has occurred under Gorbachev. Most top leaders of Soviet economic institutes have been replaced by a new team of younger economists with an apparent mission to produce the kind of innovative thought consistent with Gorbachev's reform program. Foremost among these is the controversial innovator and apparent Gorbachev favorite, Abel Aganbegian. Another notable change was the ouster of Nikolai T. Glushkov as the Chairman of the State Committee for prices. Glushkov had been one of the most outspoken critics of reform. Also of major significance was the removal of Gosplan Chief Nikolai Baibakov, whom many Soviet officials have identified as a major impediment to reform, and Richard Kosolapov, the chief editor of the main party journal *Kommunist*. Kosolapov had publicly differed with Gorbachev on questions of reform and had continued to take a conservative editorial line. The replacement of Premier Tikhonov early on, and his retirement from the Politburo, removed a principal rallying point for bureaucratic resistance to Gorbachev's program.

Western specialists on the Soviet Union are in the process of trying to assess the importance and potential impact of Gorbachev's programs and initiatives for reforming the economy. The critical question being debated is whether these programs represent any fundamental change in the structure of the Soviet economy and, if so, whether they will have an impact on its performance.

Measuring the Changes

One method of gauging the extent of the changes in the USSR is to compare them with the reforms that have taken place in Hungary. The Hungarian economy has undergone major systemic change over the last 30 years—probably the most extensive of any socialist system in the world. Some analysts, in fact, are of the opinion that the Hungarian economy has become, or is close to becoming, a system of "market socialism." The article by Janos Kornai, the prominent Hungarian economist and member of the Hungarian Academy of Sciences, presents an excellent analytical framework for making such a comparison. Using Kornai's model, the current changes in the Soviet economy have been measured against those in Hungary (see Table 2).

The comparison of the reform process in the two countries clearly reveals that the changes to date in the USSR have been relatively minor. Of course, the Hungarian reform process has been evolving for decades whereas Gorbachev has been in power for two years. Nonetheless, the changes in the Soviet Union pale in comparison with those in Hungary across practically the whole spectrum of the economy.

The assessment of Gorbachev's reforms is more stark considering the fact that the Hungarian reforms apparently are not as "radical" as they appear at first blush. According to Kornai, the reforms in Hungary have gone only halfway. In his words, state-owned firms face only "soft budget constraints"—that is, the state provides permanent subsidies, favorable tax conditions, and bail-out credits to ailing enterprises—and central authorities continue to dominate enterprise activities and operations.

> The Hungarian economy is a symbiosis of a state sector under indirect bureaucratic control and a nonstate sector, market oriented, but operating under strong bureaucratic restrictions.[19]

The Consensus of Western Experts

The overwhelming consensus of Western experts who have analyzed the changes in the Soviet economy under Gorbachev is that they do not constitute much real reform. Gertrude Schroeder, a Western expert on economic reform in the USSR, states that "the measures . . . are neither radical nor a reform, for they do not *re*-form (restructure) the economic system in any essential way." According to Schroeder:

> If Mikhail Gorbachev yearns to rank with Vladimir Lenin and Joseph Stalin as great reformers of the Soviet economic system, he will have to come up with a radically different blueprint from that underlying the measures he has sanctioned thus far. As of this writing, the treadmill continues.[20]

Ed A. Hewett's preliminary assessment of the Gorbachev agenda for change is also pessimistic. According to Hewett, "even at this early stage Gorbachev's reforms are already burdened with potentially fatal flaws." He identifies these flaws as (1) the regime's continuing effort to push too hard for high rates of output growth at the expense of product innovation; (2) the conflicting signals being given to ministers—exhorting them to refrain from interfering in the affairs of enterprises but holding them ultimately responsible for the performance of those enterprises; and (3) the continuance of the old, very complicated organizational structure of the central bureaucracy.[21]

Economist Vladimir Kontorovich maintains that "it is not enough to introduce some (market) elements into the command economy; the entire system must change." According to Kontorovich, the ideological and political baggage of 70 years of Soviet power represents a built-in mechanism in the USSR to ensure that the economic system is not changed.[22]

A Closer Look at the Reform Debate

A deeper analysis of the current debate in the USSR yields some sobering insights. For one thing, only a relatively small portion of the discussion centers around core economic questions. Gorbachev has been harshly critical of Soviet economists on numerous occasions, in fact, for not going far enough in exploring and analyzing new methods and new techniques and in failing to come up with an adequate blue print for change. Rather, the central focus of the debate is on political

Table 2

Comparing Soviet and Hungarian Economic Reforms

Sector of the economy	Hungary	USSR
Industry		
Selection of top managers	Since 1985, elected directly or indirectly by employees. (The state has formal or informal veto power.)	Appointed by the Party.
Determination of output	Short-term plans determined by firms. (The state makes "informal" requests.)	Determined by state planners.
Determination of inputs	Mixture of market contracts based on negotiations and on "gentlemen's agreements" based on reciprocal favors. (There are still informal quotas and restrictions.)	Centrally allocated.
Determination of prices	Some set administratively; most determined by firms in accordance with strict rules or with formal or informal approval of authorities. Prices still not the decisive factor in firm's decisions.	Most are set administratively by the state.
Determination of wages and employment	Mandatory employment quotas abolished but formal and informal restrictions on hiring remain. Workers free to change jobs. Wage restrictions remain in state firms.	Wages set by the state. Firms are to be given additional latitude in paying bonuses. Impact and importance unclear. Workers free to change jobs.
Credit	Highly centralized monetary system. Credit rationed by administrative authorities. Resolution in the works to establish state-owned, but competing, commercial banks. Bond trading now legal, but size of market is small.	Highly centralized monetary system; credit rationed by administrative authorities. No money or capital markets.
Investment	Highly centralized. About one-fifth financed by firms' own funds.	Centrally determined. In the future, renovation of capital assets is to be financed from firms' profits

Agriculture		
Cooperatives	Firms can sell to the state or do their own marketing. Central planning of farm production abolished in 1966. Substantial autonomy in using own profits.	Centrally controlled through production and input quotas. Gorbachev's concept of *prodnalog* allows sale of a percentage of planned production to cooperatives
State farms	Can sell to the state or do own marketing. Central planning of farm production abolished in 1968.	Centrally controlled through production and input quotas. Gorbachev's concept of *prodnalog* allows sale of a percentage of planned production to cooperatives.
Private plots	Prices determined in marketplace. No restrictions on output.	Operates on a free market basis. Role of private farming declining. Although restrictions on private agriculture now relatively relaxed, private producers have lowest claim on state resources.
Other Sectors		
Nonagricultural cooperatives	Similar freedoms and restrictions to state-owned firms but more subject to market forces and less sheltered by state. Long-standing intellectual backing for cooperatives as a basic form of enterprise ownership.	Virtually nonexistent (mostly abolished in 1961).
Private Sector		
A. Formal	Minor segment of economy. Officially licensed by the state. Employment restricted to family members plus 7 other employees.	Negligible segment of economy.
B. Informal	Deliberate effort to legalize or be tolerant of these activities. May add 20% to Hungarian GDP. Done mostly by "moonlighters." Much of the output produced is for household's own use. Wide continuum of legal and illegal activities.	Illegal second economy believed to contribute significant portion of Soviet GNP. New law on private initiative promulgated. Impact it will have unclear, but restrictions are not likely to lead to an increase in private activity soon.

and social aspects of change. Most prominent has been T. I. Zaslavskaia, a sociologist from the USSR Academy of Sciences Economic Institute at Novosibirsk, who calls for the democratization of Soviet society.

Most of the economic initiatives that have been proposed have been authored by economists who fall into the category of reformers Hanson calls "rationalizers." "Rationalizers" are defined as economists who want central planning maintained but in a simplified and streamlined way. Few are "marketeers," that is, favor abolishing most of the central ministries, wholesale trade in producer goods rather than centralized supply, elimination of plan targets, and at least some decentralized price-setting.[23]

A second fact that stands out is the striking similarity between the current reform measures and previous efforts to restructure the economy—especially the Kosygin reforms of 1965. According to Schroeder, the current Soviet leadership has concluded that the 1965 reforms were sound and that their failure lay in a lack of vigorous implementation.[24] It seems clear, however, that the 1965 reforms failed because they did not remedy the structural weaknesses of the Soviet system—a perverse incentive system, overly rigid central planning, and the inadequacy of the pricing system. The current set of initiatives, mostly a carbon copy of previous measures, appear to be similarly flawed.

A Rocky Road Ahead

Gorbachev has made redressing Soviet economic problems the hallmark of his regime. His game plan includes a two-front assault—better economic policies and reform of the economic system. On the first of these fronts, his economic policies, Gorbachev faces a number of major obstacles at home and abroad which will limit the gains in performance that can be achieved.

• In the years ahead, the Soviets will have to contend with resource problems more severe than those faced by any postwar regime. The annual number of new entrants to the work force during the second half of the 1980s, for instance, will be the lowest in decades, and the cost of exploiting fuels and raw materials is growing higher and higher.

• International events probably will work against Soviet interests in the years ahead. The world price of oil, for example, while it may rise somewhat, is likely to remain low enough to keep Moscow's hard-currency purchasing power depressed in the years ahead.

• Political and economic realities at home are likely to delay, perhaps even thwart, the implementation of the regime's policies and programs.

Progress on the second front is also likely to be slow. Historically, attempts at reform in the USSR have met with tremendous political opposition. Gorbachev's programs are no different. Dissatisfaction with one aspect or another of his initiatives is present at almost every level of Soviet society.

• A broad spectrum of the *apparat* opposes moving too far in reforming the economy on grounds that economic decentralization would threaten a loss of centralized political control by the party. Hence members at all levels of the CPSU can be expected to oppose measures they perceive as moving too far in that direction.

• A major decentralization would threaten the jobs, status, power, and privileges of thousands of officials running the economy. Hence, bureaucrats in central planning organs such as Gosplan, Gossnab, and the State Price Committee are likely to oppose such measures vigorously.

• The specter of unemployment, inflation, and the emergence of enduring divisions within Soviet society are being used by Party ideologues to lobby against reform measures. These are thorny issues that go to the heart of the basic tenets of socialism.

One indication that Gorbachev is encountering opposition is the tone of his speeches. They clearly have become more harsh and scolding, reflecting his frustration with the pace at which his programs are being implemented and with the people that oppose them. From his speech to the January 1987 plenum:

> We see that change for the better is taking place slowly, that the cause of reorganization is more difficult and the problems which have accumulated in society more deep-rooted than we first thought. . . . There still is some misunderstanding in society and in the Party of the complexity of the situation. . . . This explains questions from some comrades about the measures that are being taken . . . in the course of the reorganization. We are often asked if we are not measuring too sharp a turn.

There is no evidence so far, however, to suggest that the opposition has evolved into major rival, and potentially dangerous, political coalitions.

Ironically, the most significant opposition to major reform could come from the Soviet population. Soviet workers have become comfortable working in an environment where job security is more or less guaranteed and where there is little pressure to work hard. For example, if the Soviets follow through with plans to base wages on employee effort, a number of shopfloor workers could lose their jobs. An article published in the September issues of the Soviet journal *Sovetskaia kul'tura* warned that rank-and-file workers will not willingly give up the existing system. Indeed, Soviet citizens are likely to view such developments as a violation of their "implicit social contract" whereby, as Soviet workers are fond of saying, we pretend to work while the government pretends to pay us.[25]

In any event, Gorbachev's call for "radical" measures to transform the economy has not been followed up with initiatives that constitute, by any realistic standards, real reform. Those measures that have been introduced or are being discussed are, to a large extent, a repeat of previous ideas that have not worked before and are not likely to be much more effective this time. Most important, as mentioned above, the range of initiatives does not adequately address the kinds of problems that are at the heart of Moscow's economic difficulties.

The regime's blueprint for "radical" economic reform, for example, calls for independently operating enterprises, for "wholesale trade" between enterprises, and for changes in the way prices are determined. But it does not call for central planning to be abolished or even significantly reduced. While annual plans are to be phased out, five-year plans will take their place. Nor does it call for the centrally directed supply system to be dismantled. Although plants will be able to obtain inputs directly from suppliers, they can only do so under the direction of the central supply network. Perhaps most important, the Soviets have shown no disposition to adopt more realistic prices—that is, prices that reflect supply and demand—and almost no attention has been given to the questions of unemployment, business failures, or the other side of the coin, high income and excess profits. Nor is there any discussion of more efficient and rational ways to allocate capital resources. The logical outgrowth of full financial autonomy for firms is the complete decentralization of investment decisions. Gorbachev has given no indication that the decentralization of investment decision-making or the formation of money and capital markets are part of his *perestroika* (restructuring) plans.

In sum, the Soviets are not likely to get the kind of results they are seeking. This is not to say that some significant progress cannot be made. But the gains in productivity required are simply too great, given the major obstacles the regime faces. At a minimum, political reform is going to have to precede economic reform. But political change will be a tough nut to crack, especially since the role of the party will have to be redefined—something that even Gorbachev will find difficult to do. The vested interests in the current system are too great and too well entrenched for change to occur quickly, if at all.

Appendix: Models of Economic Reform

Soviet officials have responded to Gorbachev's call for economic reform by examining other socialist models of industrial reform. Their attention has focused on three primary countries: Hungary, China, and East Germany.

Hungary

The country with the longest history of reform is Hungary, where practical reform measures began in 1956–57 with the abolition of compulsory deliveries in agriculture. The reforms were expanded intermittently in subsequent years and now include—in the industrial sector—the abolition of short-term mandatory planning, more freedom in determining prices, the abolition of mandatory employment quotas, and some decentralization of investment decisions. In agriculture, cooperatives—the largest agricultural sector by far—and private farmers are free to sell their output on the open market. Of particular significance has been the growth of the private sector in Hungary—it may add according to Kornai, 20 percent or more to the officially recorded GDP.[26]

East Germany

The present version of centralized industrial management and planning in East Germany is closer to the Soviet system than to the systems of contemporary Hungary and China. The main characteristics of the East German system are the *Kombinate*, or industrial "combines." Under this system, enterprises are grouped into "combines" to provide greater focus on production tasks, promote economies of scale, reduce administrative redundancies, and streamline decision-making. Combine directors are granted broad powers to manage but are constrained by centrally imposed written guidelines. They are held personally responsible for the combine's performance.

China

The most recent Communist reform model is China. Launched in the late 1970s, the Chinese reform drive initially focused on agriculture. The farm sector was made a more market-oriented agricultural economy—communes were dismantled and families were allowed to rent farmland and to make their own production decisions. Since that time reforms have been expanded to the industrial sector. Measures have been approved to reduce the extent of central planning and the role of the government and party in day-to-day business operations. In addition, prices of nonstaples and some consumer goods are no longer determined by the central authorities.

Notes

1. For a discussion of the recent performance and problems of the Soviet economy see the joint CIA/DIA report DDB-1900-122-86, *The Soviet Economy under a New Leader*, Washington, D.C., July 1986.

2. The construction of these plans evidently was a difficult and contentious process. This apparently was due to Gorbachev's insistence that the plan reflect his reordered investment priorities and commitment to rapid economic progress. The regime remanded the 1986-90 Plan to Gosplan for revision several times to the 27th Party Congress in February and March 1986.

3. N. I. Ryzhkov, "On the Basic Guidelines for the Economic and Social Development of the USSR for 1986-1990 and the Period through the Year 2000," report to the 27th Party Congress as published in *Pravda*, March 4, 1986, pp. 2-5.

4. The Kremlin has already commissioned a number of "experiments" that allow enterprises greater latitude in the wages they pay workers. For example, contract brigades are being used in agriculture, construction, and some sectors of industry. These are small groups of workers whose earnings depend on fulfillment of contractual obligations to management.

5. The discipline campaign was introduced by Andropov in late 1982. It was intended to prevent violations of work rules—such as taking time out of the work day to shop—to enforce tighter discipline in management and to punish corruption.

6. In May 1985, the Gorbachev regime announced the implementation of a program to curtail alcohol abuse in the Soviet Union. The USSR currently has the highest levels of hard-liquor consumption in the world, and the economic and social costs are high. For example, according to Soviet statistics, 60 percent of unauthorized absences in factories and 25 percent of industrial accidents can be traced to alcohol abuse. This contributes to a loss in the productivity of workers estimated at 10 percent or more. For a discussion of the alcohol problem in the USSR, see Vladimir Treml, *Alcohol in the USSR* (Durham, N.C.: Duke University Press, 1982).

7. In his report to the Central Committee in June 1986, Gorbachev castigated past "serious errors" in investment policies, saying there was no justification for reductions in investment increases five-year period after five-year period. The 1986-90 Plan calls for total investment to increase by about 5 percent a year, over against a 3.5 percent per year growth during 1981-85.

8. Soviet plans call for the retirement rate of all fixed assets to increase from 1.8 percent in 1985 to 3.2 percent by 1990; machinery and equipment retirement rates are to be raised from 3.2 percent in 1985 to 6.2 percent by 1990.

9. Responsibility for monitoring the quality of output produced has been assigned to a new organization—the State Acceptance Organization (*Gosudarstvennaia Priemka*) under the State Committee for Standards. Under this new system, inspectors will be assigned to civilian plants to monitor quality standards.

10. For a discussion of Moscow's investment policies in the 12th Five-Year Plan period, see Robert E. Leggett, "Moscow's Investment Policy: The Key to Gorbachev's Program for Revitalizing the Soviet Economy," Joint Economic Committee, U.S. Congress, forthcoming.

11. Janos Kornai, "The Hungarian Reform Process: Visions, Hopes, and Reality," *Journal of Economic Literature*, December 1986, p. 1691.

12. The most ambitious experiment to date, one that markedly increases enterprise autonomy, has been conducted at the Togliatti Automotive Plant and the Frunze Machine-Building Production Association. The experiment suspends state financing and gives managers more responsibility in planning and control over earnings and spending. Plant managers are allowed to make organizational changes, adjust salaries, develop new production models, and, most important, set standards for evaluating performance. They are permitted to use, for example, almost half of the plant's profits and hard-currency earnings to finance operations and to purchase Western equipment.

13. Aganbegian discussed this three-stage agenda in an interview appearing in *Nedelia* (Moscow), no. 1, January 1987, pp. 2–6. The draft law on State enterprise rights appeared in *Pravda*, February 8, 1987, pp. 1–3.

14. *Sobranie Postanovlenii Pravitel'stva SSSR*, no. 18, 1986.

15. There are three basic channels of food distribution in the USSR: (1) state stores run by the Ministry of Trade and Gosagroprom; (2) cooperative enterprises and organizations; (3) collective farm markets. In his speech to the 27th Party Congress, the Chairman of the Central Union of Consumer Cooperatives stated that 3 billion rubles would be allocated during the 12th Five-Year Plan to improve cooperatives' logistic base—as much as had been allocated for the past 20 years combined.

16. Gorbachev described this scheme as a contemporary version of Lenin's tax in kind (*prodnalog*). This was a measure introduced in 1921 that put an end to the policy of confiscating all farm surpluses and opened the way for the New Economic Policy (NEP) with its more tolerant attitude toward private enterprise and markets.

17. *Sobranie Postanovlenii Pravitel'stva SSSR*, no. 10, 1987 and no. 11, 1987.

18. *Pravda*, December 19, 1986.

19. Kornai, *op. cit.*, p. 1715.

20. Gertrude E. Schroeder, "Gorbachev: 'Radically' Implementing Brezhnev's Reforms," *Soviet Economy*, forthcoming.

21. Ed. A. Hewett, "Reform or Rhetoric: Gorbachev and the Soviet Economy," *The Brookings Review*, Fall 1986, pp. 13–20.

22. Vladimir Kontorovich, "Lessons in the 1965 Soviet Economic Reforms," December 1986, unpublished.

23. Philip Hanson, "On the Limitations of the Soviet Economic Debate," Center for Russian and East European Studies discussion papers, General Series 2, University of Birminghan, England.

24. Schroeder, *op. cit.*, p. 11.

25. For a discussion of the population's reaction to Gorbachev's initiatives see Elizabeth Teague, "How Widespread Is Popular Dissatisfaction with Gorbachev's Policies?" Radio Liberty Research Bulletin, no. 52 (3413), December 1986, p. RL 472/86.

26. Kornai, *op. cit.*, p. 1707.

F. I. Kushnirsky

Soviet Economic Reform
An Analysis and a Model

I. Introduction

Over the past twenty years, no single event in the Soviet economy has
drawn as much attention from Western analysts as did the 1965 economic reform.[1] Subsequent developments were less exciting. Although
planners quietly worked on improving their methodology in the 1970s,
the decade was, as the Soviet press puts it now, stagnant. In 1973 a
restructuring of the middle level of management and a major price
revision for machines and equipment took place. In 1979 a resolution
on change in planning methodology, stressing the normative approach
to planning, was passed. If the number of publications on the Soviet
economy were to be a measure of excitement, that number should have
dropped in the 1970s. The rapid leadership turnover of the early 1980s
stimulated a new rise in the publications, particularly since Gorbachev
has come to power.

Among the notable Gorbachev initiatives are the anti-alcohol and
anti-corruption campaigns, the shake-up of the bureaucratic establishment, the introduction of elections for plant management, reform of the
wage system in industry, the stiff prosecution of unearned income,
legalization of small-scale private manufactures and services, a self-
financing provision for a group of enterprises, state quality control at
industrial firms, decentralization of foreign trade operations, and the
approval of certain joint ventures with capitalist firms. The new provisions are being pursued with different degrees of rigor, and some may
be incompatible. The incompatibility arises because Gorbachev had

The author teaches at Temple University.

probably solicited proposals from three special-interest groups: the leadership of the economic departments of the Central Committee, the experts from Gosplan, and the Council of Ministers and selected academic economists. Although all the proposals are subject to the approval of the departments of the Central Committee, that they are identified with different groups might contribute to their inconsistency.

These, as well as forthcoming Gorbachev initiatives, will have different impacts on the Soviet economy. While most of them continue the good old planning tradition, there is also an attempt to shake up the ossified society and to introduce some institutional changes. It may therefore be useful to analyze the pros and cons of those measures and to theorize about their potential outcomes. In this respect, the purpose of this paper is twofold and is in two parts. First, I look at the most visible alterations in the Soviet economic system from the standpoint of their feasibility and the difference, if any, they can make. Among the issues discussed are those related to methodology, incentives, and technological change. Second, I suggest a model of Soviet economic reform. No one, of course, can formulate the sufficient conditions for reform, which is a long-term process. But I believe that, for the reform to succeed, some fundamental changes in the Soviet socioeconomic system must be introduced. The worker equity-ownership program, discussed below in detail, is at the heart of the model I propose.

II. The New Economic Mechanism

Alterations in Planning

An economic experiment was started in five selected ministries in 1984–85 and thereafter expanded in scale (*shirokomasshtabnyi eksperiment*). It is now a reality for all nonagricultural production enterprises. Since 1987 a new economic mechanism (NEM) has been introduced for industrial ministries, construction, transport, communication, and most of the paid services. The enterprises of those ministries will receive their plan assignments and will report the results in accordance with the indicators tested in the experiment. While the intent of the 1965 economic reform was clear, the purpose of the NEM has been widely misunderstood. Both have aimed at the reduction of the number of centrally planned targets, but they used different tools. In 1965 some indicators were dropped from the list of centrally planned targets, with the firm allowed to make an independent determination of those dropped. The assumption was that, in order to report success in the planned targets such as, for example, profit, the firm would have to improve performance in the unplanned indicators such as cost. However, the assumption proved to be wrong. It was possible to use the loopholes to raise profits without lowering costs or to raise individual wages without increasing productivity.

The NEM approaches the same problem from a different angle. It reduces the number of targets planned directly and determines the other targets indirectly, as functions of certain success indicators. Special normative functions are mostly built for financial flows: wages, incentive funds, and payments to the state budget and to the ministry. Each of these variables may be computed with the use of normative coefficients that tie them to the indicators such as profit, productivity, and output. Thus, the firm's annual wage bill is the sum of a base value and an additional fund. In one of the several versions, the base value is found as the wage bill of the previous year corrected by the rate of productivity growth, and the additional fund depends on the rate of output growth. Both rates are multiplied by a normative coefficient of the wage growth. If combined in one step, the computation of both components of the wage fund is as follows:

$$W = B(1 + \alpha(\ell_a - \ell_p))(1 + \alpha \cdot r), \qquad (1)$$

where W, B, α, ℓ_a, ℓ_p, and r equal, respectively, the firm's annual wage fund, its wage fund in the previous year, the normative coefficient of the wage growth per one percent of the output growth, the average actual rate of productivity growth since the beginning of the five-year period, the average planned rate of productivity growth since the beginning of the five-year period, and the rate of output growth in the current year, respectively. Table 1 illustrates the computation.

Inserting the data in formula (1) yields the wage fund:

$$W = 10,000(1 + .5(.02 - .03))(1 + .5(.04) = 10,149$$

Hence, the firm's wage fund rises by 149,000 rubles in the current year.

Similar normative coefficients are applied to three funds. The sum of those three funds is the firm's retained profit. The funds are for production, science and technology, for material incentive, and for social and residential construction. Since the experiment's outset in

Table 1

Data for the Computation of the Firm's Annual Wage Fund

Indicator	Notation	Value
Wage fund in the previous year (thousand of rubles)	B	10,000
Average actual rate of productivity growth since the beginning of the five-year period (%)	ℓ_a	2
Average planned rate of productivity growth since the beginning of the five-year period (%)	ℓ_p	3
Rate of output growth in the current year (%)	r	4
Normative growth of the wage fund per one percent of the output growth	α	.5

1984 the levels of all of the normative coefficients and the format of computation have undergone alterations. The firms' management has generally been supportive of the normative approach because that way they could get higher wages and bonuses than they could when the total wage bills and bonuses were fixed in the plan. The outcome, of course, depends on the magnitude of the normative multipliers.

Another characteristic of the NEM is its emphasis on physical, rather than value, output indicators. Some firms had been surpassing plan targets in money terms, but they were underdelivering real goods and services. The authorities were not pleased, and they introduced new success indicators. Since the start of 1987, all industrial enterprises are subject to the new indicators. This time both total output and specific delivery targets (*obiazatel'stva po postavkam*) matter. The purpose of this measure is to force the firms to pay attention to all the items of the production plan. The formula used is as follows. The actual sales revenue for each product is compared with its planned value and, if it is less than planned, the difference is subtracted from the actual value. The percentage of the production plan met is then found as the ratio of the total corrected actual sales revenue to the planned sales revenue. Table 2 illustrates the computation. The firm manufactures goods A and B, with planned and actual sales revenues as indicated. Since the delivery plan for commodity A is not met, the discrepancy of 3 million rubles (10 minus 7) is subtracted from the actual revenue, thus yielding the corrected value of 4 million rubles. As a result, the firm falls short of meeting the delivery plan, with a .96 index (24 divided by

Table 2

Illustration of New Sales Revenue Success Indicator

Commodity	Planned sales revenue	Actual sales revenue	Corrected actual sales revenue
A	10	7	4
B	15	20	20
Total	25	27	24

25), showing a deficiency of four percentage points. Conversely, if this peculiar method were not applied and if full actual sales revenue counted, the firm would surpass the production plan by 8 percentage points (27 divided by 25).

The producer is rewarded for meeting the delivery plan and penalized otherwise. Thus, during the 1984–85 experimental stage, firms would lose 3 percent of their material incentive fund for each percentage point of deficient delivery but would receive an added 15 percent of the fund if the plan were met.[2] Since the authorities do not want any deliveries but those requested by the plan, their intent is easy to understand. Yet the question is whether the formula hits the target. As the Central Statistical Administration reports, formulas do not do miracles; in 1986 every fourth producer violated the "delivery discipline."[3] And this despite the fact that numerous loopholes are provided and, as a result, most violations remain unreported. (It is all right, for example, to alter a delivery contract in the planned period or to seek a written agreement from the user on the substitution of items.) This approach stimulates the producer to reduce the list of buyers and to secure an easy delivery plan, and, therefore, it further strengthens the seller's position in the market. Even if there are no significant changes in the Soviet economic model, it is hard to believe that the planners will retain the delivery-target approach in the next five-year plan.

The idea of self-investment and self-financing (*samofinansirovanie*) is not new to Soviet economic planning; yet it has begun to be implemented in industry only recently. The first experiments, conducted in the instruments industry, were not well organized. In 1985–86 planners experimented with two large enterprises—AvtoVAZ and the Sumy machine-building plant. The experiment was expanded in 1987 when seven ministries and 37 enterprises of other ministries were picked to become a part of the NEM. Of the ministries, automotive, chemical machinery, and instruments have already had some experience with self-investment, and four others—petroleum and chemical, light, marine and trade—have not. Unlike other experiments, a switch from the firm level to the ministry level makes a difference for self-investment, since, in every Soviet industry, there are firms that make profits and there are firms that lose money. For this reason, the scope of the new experiment will be more limited than the one conducted by the single firms.

The self-investment experiment is built on the distribution of profit in accordance with fixed normative coefficients. The difference between this experiment and the general normative approach of the NEM is in who acquires the residual profit—the firm or the state budget. The general provision is that what the firm pays to the state budget and to the ministry and how it forms its three funds must be in accordance with certain normative percentages; the rest of the profit accrues to the state budget. In the self-investment case, payments to the budget and the ministry come first, and the residual profit in excess of the three funds (production, social, and material incentives) is retained by the firm. Because of the residual part that the firm may control, the firm theoretically becomes more interested in making a higher profit.

There is a cost to the firm for its greater control over profit. The firm will have to finance its investment, or at least part of it, from its own sources. Soviet economic planning discriminates among three types of investment, in accordance with its use—technological modernization, renovation and expansion, and new construction. In the early experiment, the first two types of projects had to be taken care of by the firm itself. In the expanded experiment. the firm will chiefly be responsible for its technological modernization and partial renovation of its existing capacities, while the expansion of existing shops may be treated the same way as a new construction. However, the individual approach to the different firms is likely to be retained, and the results are likely to depend on the importance of their industry and the level of profits made.

The idea of self-investment *per se* is healthy. Yet there are many impediments in the way of the program. One of the most visible is the broad distribution of profits, from the lucrative ones in instrument-making or electronics to the negative ones in coal production. (Since there are no mechanisms of flexible pricing in the Soviet economy, price reforms may narrow the distribution, but only in the short run.) In order to cope with the varying profit rates of their firms, the ministries differentiate the normative rates of payments to the state budget and to the ministry's centralized fund. The result is discrimination against more productive firms. For example, at the ministry's discretion, the firm will make an annual payment for its capital stock in the range of between 2 and 10 percent of its capital value, depending on the level of its profitability.[4] Firms with abnormally low profits will be freed from payment. Evidently the ministry first computes all the necessary payments and then, on this basis, derives the normative multipliers. This is not the intent of the experiment. What could one expect? The ministry is responsible for having its firms meet plan targets. It is not responsible for changing the system. Under the existing conditions, the experiment would be more successful if carried out only by the profitable enterprises of the different industries, rather than by the ministries as a whole.

In 1987 a system of state quality control (*gospriemka*) was introduced for most manufacturing industries. The emergence of this element of the NEM was not expected then, since the experimental stage that began at several plants in 1985 was supposed to involve additional firms more gradually. There are standards (*gosti*) in the Soviet Union for most goods designed for mass production. The job of the standard is to instruct the producer by specifying certain characteristics of quality and by quantifying them. When a product does not meet the standard, it is considered defective, even though, as in the case of a machine, it may actually work. Let us call this type of poor quality the first type. On the other hand, for different reasons, in the Soviet economy there are thousands of products of inferior quality produced in accordance with the standards. Let us call this type of poor quality the second type.

The task of *gospriemka* is to combat the first type. State quality control was introduced because of the inability of plant quality-control units to prevent the mass production of defective products. Plan and quality do not get along well. As the director of the Moscow watch factory complains, they have to turn out watches of inferior design to meet the production plan targets.[5] He adds that, from society's standpoint, it would be better to have fewer watches but of a better quality. (Such talk by a highly placed manager would have been viewed as heretical in the pre-Gorbachev era.) Thousands of firms are in a situation similar to the watch factory's, and frequently they violate the standards. Among the reasons for this, inadequate supplies seem to be the most important. But what is wrong with the producer who is the first in the production process? Under existing circumstances, if a significant part of a plant's output were rejected as defective, the quality controllers would jeopardize their wages as well as those of their fellow workers and managers. Being a part of the enterprise structure, they simply could not do so. The *gospriemka* units are subordinated to Gosstandart, not plant management, and they are in a position to act much more independently.

As could be expected, there have already been some serious conflicts between the state controllers and the affected workers. In the Soviet press and even in Gorbachev's speech, threats of work stoppage are mentioned.[6] Nevertheless, the introduction of state quality control is a correct move that should have been made long ago. It will indicate to plant managers and workers that the authorities are at last serious about product quality. It may also provide a useful lesson to the authorities that they cannot now have both acceleration of economic growth (*uskorenie*) and improvement in product quality. Yet, as indicated above, the state quality-control system addresses only the first type of poor quality, i.e., the production of substandard goods. Unlike his predecessors, Gorbachev may realize that no standards and quality control can substitute for the consumer's judgment. The Soviet state quality control system is another illustration of the fact that the provisions aimed at further centralization are more appropriate for the Soviet economic model than those aimed at decentralization.

New Incentives

The NEM will also incorporate some new incentives. For that purpose, greater wage differentials are promoted, and limited private activities in manufacturing and services have been legalized. A revision of the wage system in Soviet industry has been going on since 1986. The motto is to fight leveling (*uravnilovka*)—which will further promote income inequality. Among the developments are revisions of employee position lists (*shtatnoe raspisanie*), introduction of more differentiated piece-work rates for blue-collar workers, lifting of the direct planning of white collar positions, specification of white-collar positions into a greater number of grades, reevaluation of the credentials of white-collar workers, easing the control of average wages for each category of workers, and the cautious letting go of excessive labor.

All these measures will give managers greater control over their employees, and this is especially crucial in the case of work evasion. So far, the lower the worker's position, the harder it has been to dismiss him. Not only is the cost of losing such a job low, but, most important, plenty of other jobs are available. Besides, managers did not have incentives to lay off workers. The reason was in the stringent control over average wages imposed in the early 1970s. Because of the existence of wage brackets and a ceiling on the average wage for every category of workers, the managers would not be able to pay more money to their best workers even if they reduced total employment and thus saved on the total wage bill. The situation has been changing rapidly. The restrictions on wage rates are much more flexible now. A Shchekino type of experiment conducted at the Belorussia railroad led to massive layoffs. The Soviet press discusses the economic and social implication of layoffs, stressing placement and retraining, and the temporariness of the discomfort.[7] Such a scenario should, however, lead to additional inflationary pressure in the Soviet economy. If a firm releases its excess labor, its total wage bill is likely to be divided among fewer workers. And those released continue receiving compensation in one form or another for at least several months. Greater personal disposable income will hence be generated, without gains in physical output.

The legalization of private, or "individual," labor is one of the most interesting and controversial of Gorbachev's initiatives. Western reporters keep informing their readership on new auto repair shops, cooperative cafes and groceries, taxi services, clothing stores, etc. Still, we should not be misled by the scope: these are still only single enterprises that operate or are preparing to operate. There are certain areas in the Soviet Union such as the Baltic republics, Transcaucasia, and Central Asia where proprietorship is likely to succeed more rapidly, and there are other areas that will need more time to adjust. For example, the southern part of the European RSFSR is better prepared for the acceptance of private activities than is the northern part.

The willingness to accept private economic activity is a function of both the differences in the success of ideological brainwashing and in standards of living. In the regions with higher living standards, there is less likely to be resentment toward "money-grubbers." Consider, for instance, the possession of personal automobiles, one of the indicators of a population's well-being. With the mean of 40 automobiles per thousand Soviet citizens in 1984, the five republics above that level were: Estonia (97), Lithuania (84), Latvia (73), Georgia (55), and

Armenia (48).[8] These republics, along with Uzbekistan, could be most successful in breeding capitalists of the Soviet type. But the attitudes of the party leadership toward these republics are biased. While the Baltic republics have been allowed some greater liberties, the anticorruption drives in Central Asia and Transcaucasia may hold back the expansion of private activities there.

The future of private business activities in the Soviet Union is hard to foresee. To the party authorities, it is a supplementary, not a central part of Soviet economic reform. Therefore, after the introductory period, the extent of the further promotion of these activities will depend upon the success of other economic and social programs. The problem of income disparity will undoubtedly become crucial in this respect. If the authorities introduce sweeping revisions in the Soviet economic model that will raise productivity and wages, there will be a need for the further growth of private businesses. If, however, wage growth in industry and agriculture is restrained by low productivity, a heavier tax burden will be imposed on marketeers in order to reduce their incomes as well as their incentives.

Technological Change and Resource Allocation

The allocation of resources under NEM is geared to the industries inducing technological change in the Soviet economy, in particular machine-building and metalworking (MBMW). Every new Soviet leader needs a solid introductory campaign, to consolidate his power and to recruit supporters. Before the all-embracing term *perestroika* (restructuring) was born, Gorbachev began with the discipline and technological modernization campaigns. If the discipline is intended to clean house, the role of the modernization is more open to challenge. No one would doubt that more technological change is better than less; but, when it comes to the allocation of resources, the question of priorities arises. One should realize that, despite the claims to the contrary, the MBMW sector was not neglected in the past. Since Stalin's industrialization, it has been the leading sector of the Soviet economy. Thus, the 1985 MBMW output was officially 98 times that of the 1940 level, whereas output in the chemical and the construction materials industries, also crucial to the technological change process, increased by 74 and 48 times, respectively.[9] While the revised effort will result in an MBMW output growth of 43 percent in 1986–90, it

Table 3

Soviet MBMW Output and Investment as a Percent of Total Industry

Indicator	1966–70	1971–75	1976–80	1981–85
Output	16.3	20.1	24.3	27.4
Investment	18.4	22.0	24.2	24.3

Sources: *Narodnoe khoziaistvo SSSR* 1980: 338 and 1985: 101, 368.

officially was 73 percent in 1971–75, 48 percent in 1976–80 and 35 percent in 1981–85.[10] The MBMW sector has always received priority treatment in investment. This can be seen by calculating MBMW's percentage shares of total industry output and investment. Table 3 does this by output shares in the last year of a period and investments over the entire five-year period.

Although, as follows from Table 3, the MBMW share of industry investment rose at a slower rate than its share of output, the investment share consistently exceeded the output share until the end of the 1970s. If the MBMW sector was well treated, and if it provided machines to the Soviet economy at growth rates greatly surpassing those for other industries, why is there criticism of the lack of technological change? Does it mean that something is wrong with the machines, or is it that the Soviet economy could not make proper use of those machines, or both? Apparently Gorbachev believes in the last explanation, yet it seems that he also believes in the need for technological modernization to cure other economic problems.

All sectors of the Soviet economy are supposed to benefit from better machines in two ways. First, since the new machines are more power-ful, versatile and precise, goods produced with those machines will be of higher quality. Second, since the new machines are more efficient there will be a switch to novel technologies that use less inputs, espe-cially metals and energy. If so, extra goods will be produced from a given amount of input. In short, Gorbachev's whole strategy of growth acceleration (*uskorenie*) counts on the availability of more and better machines. Bearing past experience in mind, the question is: to what extent is this expectation realistic? The first information on the output of MBMW products since the start of the program is already available. Table 4 summarizes growth indices for 1986 and the first quarter of 1987.

To obtain an overall picture of plan fulfillment for the products in

Table 4

Growth Indices for the MBMW Output

Product	1981	1st Quarter 1987
Turbines, millions of kilowatts	95	66
Turbine generators, millions of kilowatts	84	82
Electric motors, millions of kilowatts	98	90
Metalworking machine tools, billions rubles	107	90
Forging-pressing equipment, millions rubles	94	86
Industrial robots, thousands	93	104
Precision instruments and automation machines, billions rubles	102	97
Computers, billions rubles	109	96
Petroleum equipment, millions rubles	97	93
Chemical equipment, millions rubles	96	91
Light and food industry equipment, billions rubles	98	88
Tractors, millions horsepower	100	95
Agricultural machines, billions rubles	99	100
Grain combines, thousands	100	103
Cattle and fodder production equipment, billions rubles	98	88
Excavators, thousands	102	92
Passenger cars, millions	101	100

Sources: Ekonomicheskaia gazeta 5, 1987: 11–12, and 18, 1987: 9.

Table 4, the data have been weighted. The percentages in total MBMW output were first found for all branches from the estimated 1982 input-output table. Then, to provide weights for several products within a branch, outputs in money terms or product breakdowns were used.[11] As a result, the rate of fulfillment of the plan for the reported products comes to 99 percent in 1986, and to 94 percent in the first quarter of 1987. Although that 1987 figure is low, it will rise later, since it is typical for the Soviet planned economy to deliver the bulk of its production in the fourth quarter. Nevertheless, the picture reflects the ever strained supplies of inputs faced by the MBMW sector. The first year is important for any five-year plan, and, on the basis of the 1986 figures, the MBMW sector is on the track for meeting its production plan targets. But is there hope for a turnabout in the quality of new machines? As Gorbachev promised (or was promised), 80 to 95 percent of Soviet manufactures will be upgraded to world market standards by 1990, and all manufactures will meet the highest standards by 1991–

93.[12] The 12th five-year plan does not, however, look promising. Authoritative evidence is provided by Goskomtsen, which prices new machines in accordance with improvements in their characteristics. Here is one of them:

> As before, technological advance chiefly proceeds not from the mastering of mostly new machines and equipment but from partial modernization of those that have already been in production. The majority of new machines and mechanisms differ from the existing ones by insignificant improvements in their characteristics, which does not permit them to be awarded a high markup for quality. Three-fourths of all the products introduced in 1986 have been awarded a markup for their characteristics and efficiency of no more than 10 percent of the wholesale price.[13]

This result is quite natural since Soviet designers and engineers could not introduce revolutionary improvements overnight. For so many years, they were oriented toward a backward technology and were isolated from the rest of the world.

Yet, in my view, the issue of feasibility is not central to the program of technological advance. Even if thousands of talented Soviet designers become ready to respond to the new requirements, the economy itself may not be ready to benefit from a new generation of machines. The Soviet press is full of stories of sophisticated equipment misused, wasted, and abandoned. According to Gorbachev, about 700,000 jobs in industry were unfilled in 1986, while the equipment was used in one shift. With the switch to a two-shift schedule going on now, the number of unfilled jobs will exceed 4 million.[14] With the shortage of labor in industry, the newly introduced machines with their greater opportunity cost may also be wasted. Perhaps the most convincing evidence of the relative importance of the human factor and machines is the experience of the private sector in the Soviet economy. The Soviet peasant, working on his plot with no machines, far surpassed the state sector in productivity and product quality. Private businesses legalized in 1987 will only be permitted to occupy uninhabitable premises and to buy obsolete equipment and unusable raw materials from the state organizations. Yet the authorities, perhaps rightly, believe that the businesses will succeed.

Since the 1930s heavy industry has always been king of the Soviet economy. No Soviet leader, including Gorbachev, has ever challenged the primacy of heavy industry. That would lead to a conflict with the military-industrial complex. Meanwhile, the so-called prime economic law of socialism declares that meeting growing consumer demands is the chief objective of socialism. But each time that the authorities have called for a greater output of consumer goods, investment first had to be made in metallurgy, or the chemical industry, or the MBMW sector. Then, they promised, production of consumer goods would flourish.

A Model of Soviet Economic Reform

That Fashionable Issue of Reform

What is economic reform in the Soviet context? At the intuitive level, it is a process whereby the Soviet economy becomes more demand oriented, rather than command oriented, and becomes more efficient. This means that the reform process involves both the consumer and the producer, something that was not even considered in previous attempts. Consequently, the consumer is now to be given much more decision-making power about what the economy will produce. The producer, in turn, is to be put in an environment promoting personal rather than collective economic responsibility for the results of the production process.

The loosening of the grip of central planning is usually interpreted as a movement in the direction of economic reform. As Kornai puts it, reform is ''change in a socialist economic system, provided that it diminishes the role of bureaucratic coordination and increases the role of the market,'' the two conditions that, to a large extent, overlap.[15] These conditions are, of course, necessary. It is impossible to imagine a normally functioning economy without market competition, as imperfect as it may be. Would these conditions be sufficient? The 1965 Soviet economic reform that reduced the number of centrally planned targets is an illustration. Despite the beliefs that the reform failed because it was sabotaged by conservative bureaucrats, most of its provisions presented no threat to and were enthusiastically received by many bureaucrats. The rather disappointing results such as growing shortages of both consumer and producer goods and the deterioration of their quality led to the eventual termination of those provisions.

One may, however, argue that the 1965 reform fell short of marketizing the Soviet material supply system. But what would marketizing achieve? On the demand side, it would not discriminate among industrial users in the sense that those who have the money will buy the inputs, and those who do not have the money will not buy. The well-known reason lies in the planned nature of production, according to which all industrial users will be provided with the funds to purchase the necessary inputs as soon as the relevant production quotas are approved for them. On the supply side, marketizing would not discriminate against the producer who sells products of poor quality since, with shortages prevailing, the Soviet producer-goods market will still remain a seller's market. A freer pricing system, with substantial price increases, would not ease the problem of shortages, because the producer's funds are automatically adjusted for input price increases (the effect that Kornai called the soft budget constraint). Since such marketizing would not eliminate the need for rationing material inputs, the centralization of rationing, according to the Soviet authorities, reduces the extent of potential favoritism and abuse. That may be correct.

As obvious as it may seem, this consideration shows that an increase in the role of the market *per se* is not sufficient for a genuine economic reform. To put it differently, the replacement of the material supply system by the market would not promote economic efficiency and, on the contrary, might further promote waste on the part of the Soviet producer. Therefore, what has to be sought are such institutional changes in the Soviet economy as will keep attempts to improve the performance of the socialist sector from falling apart, as such attempts have in the past. At the heart of these institutional changes, in my view, should be the fundamental issue of property ownership.

Conservative forces in the Soviet economy may well realize that the legalization of private small-scale manufacturing and services will improve the supply of consumer goods and, hence, living standards. They may even agree to pursue such legalization to the extent prevailing now in the Hungarian or the Chinese economies. But none of these economies has answered the question of how to improve the socialist sector. The Soviet experiences of the 1920s demonstrated that the coexistence of socialist and private sectors created two economic classes of the society—poor industrial workers and prosperous proprietors. On the one hand, wage growth for industrial workers was impeded by their low productivity; and, on the other, the superiority of products in private markets guaranteed the success of proprietors. As a result, the poor consistently got poorer, and the rich, richer. To solve the dilemma, Stalin crushed the private sector along with the proprietors, a step that probably saved the socialist sector from collapse.

It is clear to many in the Soviet Union that attempts to improve economic performance within the existing rigid bureaucratic system will have limited success. Opinions, however, differ on what could and should be done. Gorbachev blames political economists for the lack of theoretical research on the Soviet socioeconomic system. Yet, what could he expect from people who were for decades confined to the justification of the advantages of the socialist over the private mode of production and who still have little freedom to say what others may see as real heresy? With or without theoretical underpinning, the trial-and-error method is in the future of the Soviets if institutional changes are to be introduced in their economic model.

The leadership in the Soviet Union is aware of the fact that the issue of socialist property is central to Soviet economic performance. They also realize that, despite all the efforts of the Soviet propaganda, "the owner attitude" (*khoziaistvennoe otnoshenie*) to socialist property has not been instilled in workers. There is no consensus, however, on how much the Soviet economy should promote the owner attitude. Gorbachev may want to go further than most of his more conservative colleagues in making the reform flavor real. It is not yet clear how far he will actually go or whether he himself knows. Most likely he has some very general idea but not a specific model in mind, and his decisions will eventually be determined both by experience with each succeeding step and by how free he will be to act.

A Worker Equity-Ownership Program

Here is the basic assumption and outline of a model of Soviet economic reform that I have to propose. Soviet workers will care about socialist property when their individual economic interests are tied to this property—that is, when they are in possession of this property not as a class but as individuals. Consequently, the pivot of the Soviet economic reform proposed here is the principle of worker equity ownership: the Soviet authorities turning over all factories and other industrial enterprises to workers on the basis of employee equity shareholding. This would apply both to enterprises currently viewed as productive (mining and manufacturing, construction, freight transport, business communications, and trade and distribution) and to enterprises viewed as unproductive (passenger transport, nonbusiness communications, services and medical care). The two big exceptions would be from the first group, agriculture, some specifics of which will be discussed below, and, from the second group, education, where continuation of the present status (free and controlled by the state) would remain essential to the Soviets.

According to the model, the production firm would be authorized to issue equity stock equivalent to its assets—basically the capital stock and working capital. All of the stock is distributed among the firm's employees in amounts related to the employee's wages and years of service, with the specific formula varying for different industries. The state would legally recognize the incorporated enterprises as independent entities with an uninterrupted life. The principle of limited liability would be introduced, so that the shareholder's maximum loss equals the amount of stock in his possession. All employees would thus become legally liable for their firm's performance. The whole thrust of the reform would be to make this liability real. With this purpose, a substantial part of workers' income should depend on their equity ownership so that, in becoming shareholders, they would participate in both profits and losses of their enterprises. Income from equity would come in the form of dividends paid out of profit annually or semiannually, at the discretion of the enterprise directors.

The board of directors would be elected by shareholders, i.e., workers of the enterprise, and would be approved by the party and bureaucratic authorities. It is unrealistic to expect that, from the very outset, the workers' input to the election process would be great, but it could eventually rise. The workers' participation in the appointing of management is generally a sensitive issue to the leadership of the "workers' state." For years, Soviet propaganda condemned the Yugoslav model of workers' councils as "revisionist," and, all of a sudden, Gorbachev spelled out a similar idea. Speaking at the January 1987 Plenum of the Central Committee, he suggested that enterprise managers be elected by workers. The suggestion has already been incorporated in the draft of a new statute of industrial enterprise that was published for discussion.[16] The workers' participation in the election process, as it is visualized now, is only cosmetic, for it is far outweighed by such provisions as the supervision of the enterprise by the party and economic bureaucracy and the principle of one-man management (*edinonachalie*). In all fairness, however, it has to be admitted that it is unprecedented in Soviet reality. Several years ago Soviet bureaucrats and technocrats could not in their worst dreams foresee that they would have to bid for election rather than elevation through the convenient nomenklatura system.

What does Gorbachev want to accomplish by introducing the election process for management? The answer may lie in his interpretation of an old Soviet idea that all decision makers should be under control both from the top (*sverkhu*), which has been implemented, and from the bottom (*snizu*), which has been declared but never implemented. The combination of the two controls at all levels of decision making is, according to Gorbachev, the essence of the new Soviet democracy. When it comes to management, the new approach is not supposed to replace the old *nomenklatura* system, but instead is to raise its efficiency. Even conservative party bureaucrats may agree that, along with a good manager, they can appoint a bad one. The idea of giving the workers some say in discriminating among managers may, therefore, be considered productive. If, however, the election process is not further expanded, and if the workers' participation remains nominal, the management bureaucracy will simply adjust to the new, less comfortable realities. That it is easy to adjust to is seen from an example, described in the press, of one of the first elections that took place in Latvia at the beginning of 1987. According to Soviet sources, the director of the ailing RAF automotive plant in Elgava was dismissed, and a new one elected. Five candidates applied for the position, and the decision was made by "the representatives of the Central Committee of the Communist Party of Latvia, the Ministry of the Automotive Industry, the city Party committee, scholars, journalists, and the delegates of the workers."[17] It is not clear what impact, if any, the workers' delegation had on the outcome of the election.

Without challenging Gorbachev's intention to make the Soviet bureaucracy more open to criticism and suggestions from the workers, the question is whether the election of management would bring any improvements in the Soviet economic performance, even if the workers had the necessary muscle. Since there is a loose connection between workers' incomes and enterprise performance, they would look for a manager who is nice and easy, and so forth. Thus, their having the power to choose could even become counterproductive. Gorbachev will not accomplish his goal simply by calling upon the workers to bear in mind the performance of their enterprise and not just the manager's personality. He needs a formula that would tie workers' economic interests to their enterprise, and any workable program would have to include at least some elements of the equity ownership as outlined in this paper.

Worker equity ownership can cut the vicious circle of Soviet economic reform. All of the previous attempts failed to decentralize economic decision making because that would aggravate the problem of the separation of ownership and control. Since, in the Soviet context, the "ownership" belongs to the state, the rigid centralization of economic decision making has been a way of keeping all ends under control. An equity-ownership program that involves all employees, including plant management, would delegate the ownership role from the impersonal state to individual workers. As a result, economic decision making could also be decentralized.

The problem of the separation of ownership and control led many Western writers to worry about the health of the capitalist corporation in the twentieth century. The driving forces of such separation have been the increasing numbers of stockholders and the growing use of voting by proxy. Yet other writers have argued that the development was not so bad after all.[18] Management increases its own return and maintains its security in office by keeping the stock share price high, i.e., by maximizing profit on behalf of the corporation. Management "owns" control, subject to being divested of it by the owners of the common stock. A variety of markets constrain management and create incentives for it to benefit shareholders; this is especially true because, as a rule, corporation managers own a chunk of the stock. The election of outside directors can also perform important functions in areas where shareholders are most vulnerable—fraud, self- serving, and excessive compensation. The outside directors, if properly picked, may provide helpful analysis in decision making, for they have a perspective different from that of the people who are immersed in the corporation's affairs.

A dissatisfied stockholder theoretically has several weapons, but practically he has few ways to fight corporate management directly. His powerful weapon is the ability to sell his shares. That may be the most crucial factor in the whole institution of equity shareholding: it is what keeps the link between ownership and control from breaking completely, and it creates a democratic environment in which every shareholder counts. This right to vote against the enterprise and its management by selling shares would, in the Soviet case, be the most difficult step, but also the most important to be implemented. One should also bear in mind a significant difference between any Soviet program of equity shareholding and that of a typical Western corporation. The corporation views its shareholders as investors who provide the necessary financing, while the Soviet equity ownership would be established as a part of the employee benefit package. What would be sought from the shareholders, in the first place, is not their money, but their increased participation in their enterprise's affairs, increased loyalty and increased responsibility for the production process.

The Soviets could study the relatively few employee-owned companies in the U.S. Somewhat more common are corporations with employee stock ownership plans (ESOP). According to the ESOP association, a Washington-based lobbying and information group, companies with such plans achieve higher growth rates than their competitors of similar size.[19] The plans have been started at nearly 8,000 companies across the U.S., about half of them in the last five years. The lobbying group may be biased, but there are some success stories. One of them is the PIE Nationwide Inc., the fourth largest trucking company, with 11,000 employees. When the troubled company asked that workers take a pay cut for shares, most converted their pay cuts to 38 percent of the stock in the company. Changes in employees' attitudes helped the company to achieve a quick financial turnabout. Other companies use ESOPs as a way to encourage employee savings as well as company ownership, issuing new shares at market or favorable prices to employees.

At the outset a Soviet program of worker equity ownership would not be flexible, due to the inevitable numerous constraints. However, there is no reason why the process should not gradually become more dynamic and far-reaching. From the inception, the worker would be compensated for the loss of his shares when he leaves the enterprise, with the formula for severance pay based on the firm's success. It is not clear whether the party leaders would ever allow full transferability of the shares. To them, there would have to be a distinction between worker shareholding, as a part of the benefit program, and a free stock exchange that they may not control and from which entrepreneurial workers could quickly enrich themselves by accumulating significant numbers of shares. It is not that there are no legally wealthy people in the Soviet Union, but their well-being is closely tied to the regime's. Successful entrepreneurs, on the other hand, would view the regime as an obstacle. This is the lesson the leadership learned from the experiences of the 1920s. However, when it comes to control, the stock market would be an easier target than small-scale private manufacturing, which the authorities have nevertheless legalized. In small businesses, transactions can be concealed, but in the stock market transactions are recorded, and on that account some of the fears of the party bureaucrats might be groundless.

The organization of the Soviet enterprise would have to be adjusted to the proposed worker equity-ownership program. If the enterprises become more market oriented, the management should be more open to input from the public. To that end, the general public, along with the workers, should be represented on the enterprise's board of directors. The representation of the workers would provide the directors, who will manage the enterprise, with feedback from their rank-and-file shareholders. Yet that representation should not be so powerful that it could affect the directors' wage policy. The Yugoslav experience of workers' councils indicates that when human beings are given the right to decide on their own wages, they tend to be generous. It is important that from the very start of a worker-ownership program long-term economic growth be emphasized over current wage increases. In the market economy, wage increases are limited by the company's competitive position, a constraint that does not exist in the Soviet case. If the Soviet economy becomes more market oriented, the lack of market competition and economic liability on the part of managers may initially lead to excessive demands for material inputs. If, in addition, prices are allowed to change in accordance with the forces of supply and demand, significant price surges could be expected. Therefore, the contribution of wages to the inflationary pressure should be reduced. With this in mind, both workers and managers should be put in a position where the growth of their income depends on dividends, rather than on wages.

Some of the Systematic Problems Addressed

For worker ownership to work, a complex of other conditions must be met. As in previous attempts at Soviet economic reform, it might be abortive if the systematic nature of Soviet economic diseases is not addressed. The workers and managers have to see that the sale of their product is not guaranteed by the mere fact of its inclusion in the plan, that they do not produce the only product available to the consumer, and that, under these conditions, they can get a fair price for their product. For these conditions to be met, the entire planning system that protects the producer from competition and decides on production, technology, prices, and sales must undergo radical changes. For a number of reasons, diminishing the scope of central planning in the Soviet economy would be a lengthy process. Yet, from the very outset, mandatory production quotas could be eliminated for thousands of products that might be supplied without intervention from the planning authorities.

As discussed earlier, the planners' control over the spending of national resources is justified, since the managers of industrial firms are not charged with any economic responsibility for such spending. With the introduction of worker equity ownership, the situation might change, so that the authorities could rely more on market self-regulating mechanisms rather than forcing one firm to produce a good and another to buy it. Production planning for strategically important goods and goods in short supply would continue, but it would be eased in the ensuing steps of the reform.

Along with the planning of important production, other functions of Gosplan would include forecasting, analysis of economic development, investment planning, and the promotion of competition among producers. Gosplan would remain the only central economic body of the government involved in production planning. The ministries would lose their supervisory and production-planning functions and would concentrate on research and development for different branches of the economy. The ministries would, accordingly, retain their research, design, and development institutes, and bureaus that would sell their services to the enterprises. In addition, those units would work on the government-sponsored projects. One of the many conditions necessary for worker equity ownership is the creation of a competitive environment in the Soviet goods markets. Even the Soviet authorities now say that the monopoly power of the producer under the protection of the plan has to be reduced. Equity ownership will not do this automatically, but it will make the workers economically interested in both raising the production and reducing the cost of inputs. That will put an upward pressure on supply and a downward pressure on demand for producer goods, thus decreasing the seller's power in the markets for those goods. The task of Gosplan, in turn, would be to encourage industrial enterprises to diversify their outputs and, whenever possible, to enter new markets.

Market competition may be a road to either success or bankruptcy. The Soviets have already realized the necessity of shutting down inefficient enterprises. Thus in 1986 an unprecedented decision was made to liquidate two research institutes—of the chemical machinery and of the machine tool industry—and to place their workers in other jobs.[20] Some Soviet economists openly admit that this is only the first step and that millions of workers will have to be released from inefficient enterprises. In addition, equity ownership may stimulate management to get rid of excessive labor and to cut other costs. But, considering social implications, it is uncertain to what extent the Soviet leaders make competition real and to what extent it would remain a game. The Yugoslav example, however, demonstrates that if the government, on the one hand, promotes market competition and, on the other hand, bails out the losers, the outcome is neither economic efficiency nor social harmony. As a matter of fact, Yugoslavia, with inflation over 100 percent and every sixth worker unemployed, has experienced about 500 walkouts annually.[21]

Although the Soviets can learn from the Yugoslav experience, they still cannot let their enterprises alone in the near future. It is one thing to close several institutes or bureaucratic bodies, and another thing to close a thousand industrial firms. As discussed above, even in a profitable Soviet industry there are many firms that are in the red, for reasons that may be exogenous to the firm. Since, along with distorted prices, there is excess demand in the Soviet producer goods markets, raising prices would not be a solution, even though some price increases are inevitable. Gosplan and the ministries are to play a crucial role in helping firms with obsolete technology improve their competitiveness in the market. Natural monopolies will have to be regulated by Gosplan.

The pricing mechanism plays an important role in different models of market socialism. The socialism part is usually represented by a decision-making "center," and the market part, by individual agents who pursue their own interests under the constraints imposed by the center. The existence of the center is justified, for example, by the fact that it determines the clearing prices and conveys them to the individual agents. But any such model is at most a good illustration of a much more multifaceted reality.[22] Aside from theoretical problems, the Soviet experience has demonstrated that the first euphoria about the use of an equilibrium or an optimization model is short lived. The reason is that usually the incentives at work distort the information upon which the solution depends and lead to unexpected results. Thus the attempts to "optimize" pricing of new machines on the basis of their projected characteristics failed because the data on potential benefits provided by the producers were inflated, and the data on costs, deflated. As a result, the last (1982) instruction on pricing reemphasized the good old cost-plus-profit principle. A similar disappointment emerged from a well-organized experiment on the use of input-output tables in planning.[23] This time the computation depended upon technological coefficients provided by the ministries. As a result, gross outputs and intermediate products came out the same as those the ministries were trying to defend before Gosplan.

The introduction of equity ownership and the creation of competitive markets in the Soviet economy would eventually end price setting by the central authorities, except for natural monopolies. Yet the road to market prices that reflect consumers' rather than authorities' preferences will be long and painful. There is no reason to expect that the Soviets could avoid the pitfalls of the Yugoslavs, Hungarians, and Chinese in whose countries the easing of price controls has contributed to inflationary growth. The lesson that the Soviets have to learn from the experiences of these countries is this: the greater the incentives and improvements brought about by the privatizing of many of the economic activities, the greater is the pressure to raise the incomes of workers in the socialist sector. The growth of the money stock that is therefore generated, in combination with lagging productivity of the socialist sector, leads to rising prices.

What About Agriculture?

As discussed above, shortages of raw materials have been one of the most serious impediments to Soviet economic growth. The worker equity-ownership program might be helpful in two ways. First, it would raise disincentives to waste inputs, since, being economically affected by the performance of their enterprises, the workers would weigh more carefully the costs and benefits of production alternatives. Second, since industries producing metals, ores, fuels and energy would also be involved in the program, higher outputs of raw materials should be stimulated. Unfortunately, no reform will work unless the supply of agricultural raw materials and produce is gradually improved. But incentives provided for industry will not work in agriculture. A different approach would be needed. Among different strata of the Soviet population there is a rare consensus that the *kolkhoz* system is bankrupt. Yet, to the older generation, dismantling it would be a political disaster. The Soviet leaders have shut their eyes to the problem and, pouring significant resources into agriculture, have attempted at least partial improvements. Extrapolating Gorbachev's criticism of the other aspects of the Soviet economy to agriculture and taking into account his experience, he must be an exception. The fact that he is silent on agricultural reform may mean that there is a limit to which he could recognize or address the problem, or it may be a result of

Table 5

Agricultural Employment and Total Soviet Employment, in Millions

Indicator	1940	1960	1985
Total civilian employment	62.9	83.8	130.3
Employment in collective farms (kolkhozy)	29.0	21.8	12.5
Employment in state farms (sovkhozy)	1.8	6.2	11.1
Combined agricultural employment	30.8	28.0	23.6
Agricultural employment in total civilian employment (%)	49.0	33.4	18.1

Source: Narodnoe khoziaistvo SSSR 1985: 390–91.

miscalculation on his part.

If there is an aspect of Hungarian reform from which the Soviets could benefit, it is the Hungarian experience with agriculture, especially in the cooperative sector. With strong material incentives, Hungarian agricultural cooperatives provided more than half of the total agricultural output in 1984.[24] While the Hungarian agricultural cooperative of the 1950s resembled the Soviet *kolkhoz,* with mandatory delivery plans at low prices, in the 1980s it is much more like an independent, market-oriented organization. For political reasons, agricultural cooperatives would be more acceptable to the soviets than private, individual farming. In addition, there is a problem in the exodus of labor from the Soviet countryside: it has reached a critical level. Table 5 illustrates employment in Soviet agriculture.

The data in Table 5 show the share of agricultural employment in Soviet total civilian employment declining from 49 to 18 percent in the 1940–85 period. Employment in *kolkhozy* has consistently declined over that period. Employment in *sovkhozy* grew until the early 1980s when it stabilized, and it fell in 1985. While such a pattern is normal for a developing country in a process of rapid urbanization, there is more to the story. There are the aging agricultural population, predominantly female labor, and broken households. Under these circumstances, independent agricultural cooperatives could become the basis for reviving the countryside and attracting skilled labor to agriculture.

To a Soviet bureaucrat, the elimination of the agricultural production plans would mean causing a famine. Yet if the cooperatives were left alone and could specialize in the products that might generate higher profits for their members, greater agricultural output would be stimulated. As a result, they could sell more both to consumers in the market and to the state procurement organizations. The property that in theory belongs to the impersonal *kolkhoz* should become the cooperative property of its members, with every member having the right to leave the cooperative and to be compensated for his share. Agricultural cooperatives should be permitted to hire workers without restrictions on the type of labor or wages paid. They should be encouraged to engage in catering, construction, and manufacturing, in particular of foodstuffs, textiles, apparel, and footwear. Cooperatives could also open their branches and stores in cities. Subcontractors could play a crucial role in organizing cooperative production. Those would be the brigades, i.e., groups of people who take care of a given production line and receive a certain percentage of the revenue generated. The brigade could be formed by members of the same family or by individuals hired on a permanent or seasonal basis. The cooperative should be free to apply its own formula to the distribution of income among its members and hired workers and to negotiate prices with the state procurement organizations. The decision to sell on the free market or to the state should be cooperatives' prerogative.

Private farming by *kolkhoz* members has helped the Soviets to survive poor crops and capricious weather and has become an integral part of their agriculture. Its importance will grow in the future. Even if the cooperatives become more efficient than *kolkhozy,* they would still specialize in certain lines of production to economize on scale. Therefore they would be interested in the diversification provided by household farming—overdue for more favorable treatment by the state. The legal restrictions on plots in private use should be eased, and those on keeping animals, including horses, lifted. In addition, agricultural machinery should become available to households. Since the notorious ban on the private ownership of "means of production" has been relaxed with the legalization of certain private manufacturing in 1987, there is no ideological reason to continue the ban in agriculture. Households should also be allowed to lease machines and vehicles, to buy seeds, and to receive other assistance from the cooperatives.

The Soviet authorities may fear that, by working hard and producing more, the peasants will turn into a wealthy class. But they have already legalized private individual manufacturing and services, which may have a similar outcome. In the past the typical response would have been to impose numerous constraints on private activities, thus killing incentives. To reverse the bureaucratic responses, economic reform should bring about the institutional changes in the Soviet economy discussed above. The intent of these measures is to put the authorities into a position where they would be concerned with raising the productivity and incomes of workers in the socialist sector, rather than reducing them in the private sector. The concept of worker equity-ownership introduced above may provide a viable solution. Along with many aspects of wages and incomes, Soviet economic reform will have to address such issues as unemployment compensation, retraining programs, labor mobility, a free market for housing, and incentives for settlement in rural areas.

Conclusion

In this paper I have analyzed the recent developments in economic reform in the Soviet Union. The legalization of "individual labor" is one of Gorbachev's decisions that is consistent with the reform mood. If Khrushchev's condemnation of Stalin damaged ideological communist doctrine, this decision may ruin its socioeconomic foundation. The whole idea of the Soviet experiment, watched with admiration by many Western idealists in the 1930s, was in the notion of collectivism and the breeding of a new type of human being who would care about the society more than himself. Now the fact that people are still individualist and selfish is openly admitted. This will be used as an answer to an unsolvable problem of supplying the population with clothes, good potatoes, or fixed faucets. Down the road, the number of obstacles faced by the new Soviet proprietorship program will grow, and we will have to watch patiently.

As to collective, not individual, activities, Gorbachev has accomplished little that could be interpreted as reform. Limited decentralization of the foreign trade operations will improve their efficiency but will not boost Soviet standing in world markets. Soviet economic problems are domestic, not international. The technological modernization program may result in a large-scale waste of scarce materials since, assuming that dramatic improvements in machines and technology are feasible, the Soviet economy is not ready to utilize them efficiently. To put it simply, better machines do not necessarily produce better goods. Probably the Soviets would be better off if they invested more in the consumer goods sector itself than in machines that would help to produce more consumer goods.

An interesting self-financing provision can illustrate the systematic nature of Soviet economic problems. The principle of a profit distribution that would enable the enterprises to finance all their expenditures, including investment, may look great on paper, but it will not work. There are thousands of Soviet firms that lose money. Not only would raising prices trigger a chain of price increases but it would be fruitless if the monopolistic power of the producer is not decreased. That could not be done without loosening the grip of central planning that is the protector against competition. But, if plan controls were lifted, the firms would have no trouble selling on the market whatever is produced, since there is excess demand for inputs. The well-known reason for the excess demand is in the collective, or ultimately the state, responsibility for inputs, which means the lack of individual liability or incentive. In short, without addressing the issue of socialist property, the problems of excess demand, rigid prices, lack of competition, and consumer sovereignty could not be addressed either.

I am suggesting a model of Soviet economic reform. At the heart of it is the program of worker equity-ownership that would tie the economic interests of Soviet managers and workers to the success of their enterprises. Equity ownership should be introduced as a part of the employee benefit package so that an essential part of the workers' income depends on their equity shareholding. The workers would participate both in the profits and in the losses of their enterprises and, as shareholders, would affect the decisions in their enterprises. (In the Yugoslav model of workers' councils, they are directly involved in decisions on wages and other matters.) Since equity ownership will make the workers more sensitive to input spending and to product quality, other measures promoting market competition, freer pricing, and greater consumer sovereignty could be easier to undertake.

Questioning Gorbachev's initiatives, we realize that at this point criticism may be cheap. We do not know who, beyond Moscow party secretary Yeltsin, unreservedly supports him at the upper echelon. Support at the lower echelons also has its limits. Many of Gorbachev's appointees probably share his ideas, but, when it comes to their new lucrative positions, they do not want to be victimized. They have already become unhappy about the prospect of elections; some of their subordinates take *perestroika* too seriously, and the press is noisy. Although there is no threat of the press becoming free, a provincial satrap may fear that one day he could face his own *Miami Herald* or *Washington Post*. All of these factors complicate Gorbachev's position and, along with what he has learned from Khrushchev's experience, make him cautious. Or is the drama not that intriguing? After all, who knows whether he is silent on agriculture because of his strategy or because of his faith in the *kolkhoz* system?

Notes

1. I would like to thank William Moskoff and Arnold Raphaelson for their help.

2. V. S. Bialkovskaia, "Ekonomicheskii eksperiment v otrasliakh mashinostroeniia," *Vestnik Mashinostroeniia* 2, 1985: 58.

3. *Ekonomicheskaia gazeta* 5, 1987: 11.

4. *Ekonomicheskaia gazeta* 2, 1987: 6, and 5, 1987: 6.

5. *Ekonomicheskaia gazeta* 11, 1987: 21.

6. M. S. Gorbachev, "O perestroike i kadrovoi politike partii, *Ekonomicheskaia gazeta* 6, 1987: 10.

7. The discussion was summarized in *Ekonomicheskaia gazeta* 19, 1987: 7.

8. Statillustratsii, *EKO* 5, 1984: 103. Because of registration in other republics, the statistics for Georgia and Armenia might underestimate car possession.

9. *Narodnoe khoziaistvo SSSR* 1985: 98.

10. N. I. Ryzhkov, *Ekonomicheskaia gazeta* 26, 1986: 13, and *Narodnoe khoziaistvo SSSR* 1985: 128.

11. Barry L. Kostinskii, "The 1982 Matrix in 1982 Prices," Draft, CIR of the U.S. Bureau of the Census, 1987; A. A. Shaporov et al., *Ekonomicheskie problemy razvitiia mashinostroeniia,* Moscow, Mashinostroenie, 1975: 10; *Ekonomicheskaia gazeta* 5, 1987: 11-12, and 18, 1987: 9.

12. M. S. Gorbachev, *Pravda,* June 17, 1986: 2.

13. L. Rozenova, "Tsena i kachestvo tekhniki," *Ekonomicheskaia gazeta* 5, 1987: 17. The ceiling on the markup for quality is 30 percent of the price.

14. M. S. Gorbachev, *Pravda,* June 17, 1986: 2.

15. Janos Kornai, "The Hungarian Reform Process: Visions, Hopes, and Reality," *Journal of Economic Literature* 24, no. 4, 1986: 1691.

16. M. S. Gorbachev, "O perestroike . . . ," p. 12; and "Proekt zakona o gosudarstvennom predpriiatii (ob "edineii)," *Ekonomicheskaia gazeta* 8, 1987: 5.

17. *Komsomol'skaia Pravda,* February 7, 1987: 2.

18. For example, Ralph K. Winter, *Government and the Corporation,* Washington, D.C.: American Enterprise Institute, 1978.

19. *Philadelphia Inquirer,* April 5, 1987: 13-G.

20. *Ekonomicheskaia gazeta* 1986: 3.

21. Mikhailo Mikhailov, "Iugoslavskii krizis i profsoiuzy," *Novoe Russkoe Slovo,* April 10, 1987: 3.

22. For analysis of the discrepancies between the reality and the assumptions of the foundational Lange model of market socialism see Kornai, *op. cit.,* 1725-28.

23. V. Vorob'ev, "O primenenii mezhotraslevogo balansa v praktike planirovaniia," *Planovoe khoziaistvo* 7, 1973.

24. Janos Kornai, *op. cit.,* 1701.

ROLF H. W. THEEN

Hierarchical Reform in the Soviet Economy The Case of Agriculture

I. The Establishment of Gosagroprom

On November 23, 1985, yet another acronym was added to the already acronym-studded vocabulary of Soviet officialdom: Gosagroprom—a term which stands for *Gosudarstvennyi agropromyshlennyi komitet SSSR*, i.e., the USSR State Agroindustrial Committee. The establishment of Gosagroprom and the attendant reorganization of Soviet agriculture constituted the first major step taken by the Gorbachev administration along the admittedly long and difficult road of *perestroika*, that is to say the restructuring of the system.[1] The shake-up of the agricultural bureaucracy was both logical and predictable—given the seriousness of the agricultural crisis in the Soviet Union, the relatively discrete character of agriculture within the Soviet economy, Gorbachev's own experience and expertise in agriculture, and the new first party secretary's evident penchant for hierarchical and personnel change in pursuit of the solution of deep-seated economic problems. Against the background of Gorbachev's emerging profile as a reform politician and the writings of reform advocates, in particular academician T. I. Zaslavskaia and B. P. Kurashvili,[2] it came as no surprise that agriculture was chosen as the touchstone of economic reform in the Soviet Union.[3] As a matter of fact, several months before the establishment of Gosagroprom, Zaslavskaia for all practical purposes had predicted that the reorganization would begin in agriculture.[4]

The creation of Gosagroprom entailed a sweeping reorganization of Soviet agriculture, which, *inter alia,* involved the abolition of five

---

The author teaches at Purdue University.

national (union-republic) ministries and one national (all-union) state committee concerned with agriculture, most of whose functions were transferred to the newly created state agency, a *de facto* superministry.[5] More specifically, Gosagroprom took over the functions of the Soviet Ministry of Agriculture (Minsel'khoz), the Ministry of the Food Industry (Minpishcheprom), the Ministry of the Food and Vegetable Industry (Minplodoovoshchkoz), the Ministry of the Meat and Dairy Industry (Minmiasomolprom), the Ministry of Rural Reconstruction (Minsel'-stroi), and the USSR State Committee for the Supply of Production Equipment for Agriculture (Goskom PTOSKh SSSR).[6]

Gosagroprom is to function as "the central organ of state management of the agroindustrial complex and, along with the Councils of Ministers of the union republics, is fully responsible for raising production, fulfilling the procurement plans for agricultural products, and securing their complete safeguarding and quality processing, as well as a significant expansion in the assortment of agricultural products."[7] The decree which created Gosagroprom also called for the establishment of corresponding state agroindustrial committees at the union republic, autonomous republic, *krai,* and *oblast'* levels, as well as appropriate reorganization at the *okrug* and *raion* levels. In addition to absorbing the functions of the five ministries and one state committee that were abolished, Gosagroprom was also given some functions of other ministries, e.g., inspection of the procurement and agricultural products—from the Ministry of Procurement (Minzag), responsibility for the primary processing of agricultural raw materials, such as wool, cotton, silk—from the Ministry of Light Industry (Minlegprom), and the examination of drafts and estimates and the determination of limits of capital investments and the financing of land improvements, etc.— from the Ministry of Land Reclamation and Water Resources (Minvodkhoz), a ministry which had earlier been subjected to reorganization.[8]

According to the text of its statute, Gosagroprom constitutes a single system consisting of the USSR State Agroindustrial Committee, its counterparts at the union republic, autonomous republic, *krai* and *oblast'* levels, the raion and okrug agroindustrial associations, the state farms (*sovkhozy*), enterprises, organizations, and institutions subordinated to them, as well as the collective farms (*kolkhozy*).[9] Along with its local organs, the system of Gosagroprom also includes the USSR Ministry of Grain Products,[10] the USSR Ministry of Land Improvement and Water Resources, the USSR Ministry of the Fish Industry

(Minrybkkhoz), and the USSR State Committee for Forestry (Gosleskhoz), as well as the Central Union of Consumers' Cooperatives (Tsentrosoiuz), whose statutory rights and functions were left intact.[11] A number of other ministries responsible for the production of capital goods and other resources for the agroindustrial complex were not brought under the direct jurisdiction of Gosagroprom, being instead directed by the statute to coordinate their work closely with Gosagroprom. In this connection, the statute named specifically the USSR Ministry of Tractor and Agricultural Machine Building (Minsel 'khozmash), the USSR Ministry of Machine Building for Animal Husbandry and Fodder Production (Minzhivmash), the USSR Ministry of Machine Building for Light and Food Industry and Household Appliances (Minlegpischemash), the Ministry of Mineral Fertilizer Production (Minudobrenii), and the USSR Ministry of the Medical and Microbiological Industry (Minmedprom). Thus, the domain of Gosagroprom is vast, but not all-encompassing. In many crucial areas linking Soviet agriculture with the Soviet industrial economy, Gosagroprom is dependent on "coordination" and cooperation.

To assure management of the agroindustrial complex as a single whole, the decree stipulates that Gosagroprom is to carry out its planning and financing in accordance with procedures established jointly with the USSR State Planning Committee (Gosplan) and the USSR Ministry of Finance (Minfin) for the ministries and state committees subordinated to Gosagroprom. With respect to the relationship of Gosagroprom to the rest of the Soviet economy, the decree states that "within the limits of its competence, Gosagroprom issues decrees (*postanovleniia*), orders (*prikazy*), and instructions (*instruktsii*), as well as directives (*ukazaniia*), which are binding for implementation by all ministries, state committees, departments, associations, enterprises, institutions, and organizations."[12] Given the past record of "cooperation" and "coordination" between the heavy industry ministries and agriculture in the Soviet Union, this provision of the statute may well represent more wishful thinking than anything else.

In terms of administrative subordination, the statute provides that the state agroindustrial committees of the union republics are subordinated both to the Councils of Ministries of the corresponding union republics and to the USSR Gosagroprom. Similarly, the statute provides that the statutes of the state agroindustrial committees of the union republics and the structure of their central apparatuses are approved by the Councils of Ministers of the corresponding union republics by agreement with the USSR Gosagroprom. The *modus operandi* of the newly created state agency was left somewhat vague by the statute: "The USSR State Agroindustrial Committee carries out the management of the industries entrusted to it, as a rule, through union republic state committees of the same name and manages associations, enterprises and organizations of union subordination directly or through organs created by it." Furthermore, "within the limits of its competence, the USSR State Agroindustrial Committee carries out the state management of the collective farms and extends assistance to the Union Council of Collective Farms in the implementation of the tasks entrusted to it with respect to questions of collective farm construction."[13]

Composition and Structure

Gosagroprom is made up of a chairman, deputy chairmen, and other members of the committee. The chairman and first deputy chairman are appointed by the USSR Supreme Soviet or, between sessions, by its Presidium, with subsequent confirmation by the USSR Supreme Soviet. The deputy chairmen are appointed by the USSR Council of Ministers. The membership of Gosagroprom also includes:

—the Minister of Grain Products;
—the Minister of Land Improvement and Water Resources;
—the Minister of the Fish Industry;
—the Chairman of the Managing Board of the Central Union of Consumers' Cooperatives;
—a first deputy chairman of the USSR State Planning Committee;
—a first deputy chairman of the USSR State Committee of Science and Technology (GKNT);
—a first deputy chairman of the USSR Ministry of Finance;
—a deputy chairman of the Managing Board of the USSR State Bank (Gosbank);
—a deputy chairman of the State Committee for Material and Technical Supply (Gossnab);
—a deputy chief of the USSR Central Statistical Administration (TsSU);
—the Minister of Tractor and Agricultural Machine Building;
—the Minister of Machine Building for Animal Husbandry and Fodder Production;
—the Minister of Machine Building for Light and Food Industry and Household Appliances;

—the Minister of Mineral Fertilizer Production;
—the Minister of the Medical and Microbiological Industry;
—the chairmen of the state agroindustrial committees of the union republics; and
—other management personnel of the USSR Gosagroprom, other ministries, departments, organizations and scientists.

Within a few weeks of its creation, Gosagroprom, in addition to its chairman, had two first deputy chairmen, 11 deputy chairmen, and 9 department heads, all appointed between November 23, 1985, and January 10, 1986, with responsibilities for the following departments: Agricultural Research; Crop Production and Processing; Food Processing; Foreign Relations and Cadres; Fruit and Vegetable Production and Processing; Livestock Production and Processing; Mechanization and Electrification; Rural Construction; and Technical Supplies and Services.[14]

To deal with questions of the basic directions of the development of science and technology, a unified technical policy, and the utilization and introduction, in production, of the latest achievements of science, technology and progressive experience, the statute provides for the establishment of a Scientific-Technical Council, in Gosagroprom, whose membership includes outstanding scientists, highly-qualified specialists, production innovators, and representatives of scientific-technical societies and other organizations, to be headed by the Chairman of the Lenin Academy of Agricultural Sciences (VASKhNIL).

Like other ministerial bodies, Gosagroprom is to have a collegium, consisting of the chairman of Gosagroprom (who chairs the collegium), the deputy chairmen of Gosagroprom (ex officio), and other executive personnel of the committee. The personnel composition of Gosagroprom and its collegium (with the exception of the ex officio members) is approved by the USSR Council of Ministers. The statute also provides for the establishment of an arbitration service within Gosagroprom to deal with economic disputes between state enterprises, institutions and organizations of the Gosagroprom system.[15]

In terms of its composition and structure, Gosagroprom, it would seem, is a fairly typical ministerial/bureaucratic organization, with rather far-flung functions and responsibilities, but ultimately under the control of the USSR Council of Ministers. According to the statute of Gosagroprom, the staff roster of its central apparatus, as well as the statutes of its structural subdivisions, are approved by its chairman. But "the Chief of the Main Administration for Planning the Social and

Economic Development of the Agroindustrial Complex, as well as the deputy chiefs of the main administrations and the departments of Gosagroprom headed by deputy chairmen of Gosagroprom, are appointed to office and dismissed from office by the USSR Council of Ministers.''[16]

Tasks and Functions of Gosagroprom

The tasks of the new state committee in charge of agriculture are spelled out in 16 paragraphs of its statute, covering more than a large page of closely-printed text. Part of the statute adds up to a fairly comprehensive summary, in Soviet terminology, of what ails Soviet agriculture in the 1980s. The statute is also a lengthy enumeration of the tasks of Gosagroprom covering the gamut of familiar prescriptions to cure these ills—from the solution of the fundamental problems related to the successful fulfillment of the Food Program and the acceleration of scientific-technical progress, the effective utilization of the existing economic production potential and the implementation of the decisions of the Party and the Government, to scientifically-substantiated planning, financing and resource provision and the securing of the balanced development of the sectors of the agroindustrial complex by regions of the country.

Gosagroprom is not only responsible for the rational distribution, specialization and concentration of production and the improvement of economic methods of management and relations based on economic accountability, but also for the increase of labor productivity, the realization of scientifically-based price formation, the introduction of the collective contract and other progressive forms of labor organization and payment—in short, measures that are in line with Gorbachev's general prescriptions for the organization of the Soviet economy. To convey some idea of the daunting scope of the tasks confronting Gosagroprom, it suffices to cite only one of the 16 paragraphs in full. Among the "main tasks" of Gosagroprom, according to its statute, are (Par. 14):

> The implementation of integrated measures for the social transformation of the village, the organization of the training and retraining of cadres with regard to the transfer of all sectors of agricultural production to the intensive path of development, the improvement of the housing, cultural and consumer conditions of the life of the collective farmers, workers, and employees, and the creation of safe working conditions.[17]

By far most of the text of the statute (more than half) is devoted to the functions of Gosagroprom.[18] If the lengthy enumeration of Gosagroprom's far-flung responsibilities conveys some understanding of the awesome tasks and challenges facing the first superministry created by the Gorbachev administration in the course of *perestroika,* the section of the statute spelling out the functions of Gosagroprom affords an insight into the thinking of the new Soviet leadership concerning "what is to be done" and suggests something about the obstacles that lie ahead.

While the distinction between tasks and functions is not readily apparent, it is clear from the statute that Gosagroprom, if anything, is more new than novel. For the most part, it represents an attempt to streamline, rationalize, and modernize agricultural production, distribution and marketing. It is also clear from the statute that Gosagroprom, at least to begin with, is supposed to solve the formidable problems of Soviet agriculture essentially within the existing framework and parameters of the Soviet economic system. The five-year plans in agriculture are to continue, as are the most important traditional indicators. The first two of the twenty-three points setting forth the functions of Gosagroprom leave no doubt that the new superministry is deeply enmeshed within the entrenched bureaucratic system of ministries and state committees—from the USSR Council of Ministers, Gosplan and the USSR State Committee for Science and Technology at the center to the Councils of Ministers and agroindustrial complexes of the union republics at the periphery. In short, at least in terms of the provisions of its statute, Gosagroprom does not have much in the way of significant autonomy vis-a-vis the established and entrenched national and regional bureaucracy. Thus, for example, in the elaboration of "the drafts of the annual and five-year plans of the economic and social development for the system of the country's agroindustrial complex," Gosagroprom has to work from "the proposals of the Councils of Ministries of the union republics, as well as the USSR ministries and departments." These plans are then submitted to Gosplan and the State Committee for Science and Technology for approval.[19] The abolition of five ministries and a state committee notwithstanding, the creation of Gosagroprom emerges as a fairly conservative move—especially given the dialectics and history of Soviet administrative reorganizations over the years. Certainly the establishment of Gosagroprom did not bring with it any startling substantive changes of the kind that were put into effect in China—with demonstrably dramatic positive results.

In addition to the rather detailed treatment of the functions of Gosa-groprom, the statute contains the usual provisions in regard to cadre policy, specifically the training and retraining of executive personnel and specialists, and grants Gosagroprom, in general terms, *nomenklatura* powers over the associations, enterprises, institutions and organizations directly subordinated to it.[20] Furthermore, the statute contains provisions for the participation of Gosagroprom in socialist competition and stipulates that Gosagroprom, by agreement with the USSR State Committee for Labor and Social Problems (Goskomtrud) and the All-Union Central Council of Trade Unions (VTsSPS), approves model provisions for wages and bonus payments of workers of state farms and other enterprises and organizations of the USSR Gosagroprom system and also guarantees their correct application.[21]

To facilitate the envisaged changes in the procedure of planning, financing, and material-technical supply for the sectors of the agroindustrial complex, the decree which established Gosagroprom also called upon the USSR State Planning Committee, the USSR State Committee for Material and Technical Supply, the USSR State Committee for Science and Technology, the USSR Ministry of Finance, the USSR State Bank, the USSR Committee for Labor and Social Problems, the USSR Committee on Prices (Godkomtsen), and the USSR Central Statistical Administration (TsSU) to reorganize the structure of their respective apparatus and to create subdivisions to secure the functioning of agroindustrial production.

Although organizational measures clearly predominate in the decree, it also included some references to more substantive aspects of Soviet agriculture. Inter alia, it endorsed "the further development of subsidiary farms of enterprises and organizations, private subsidiary farms of citizens, collective gardening and truck farming as integral parts of the food complex." Furthermore, the decree also endorsed "the broad introduction of the collective contract and economic accountability in all production links, as well as improved financing and credit extension."[22] These provisions of the November 23, 1985 decree found reflection in the statute of Gosagroprom, which stipulates that the USSR State Agroindustrial Committee "promotes the development of private subsidiary farms of citizens, collective gardening and truck farming, extends assistance to the subsidiary farming of enterprises, institutions and organizations in the acquisition of young breeding cattle, high-quality seeds, planting stock, and fertilizers, as well as in the provision of veterinary and other services for them. It promotes the development of subsidiary factories and small-scale industries in agricultural enterprises."[23] Clearly, the "privatization" of agriculture in the Soviet Union was not a major consideration in the November 1985 reorganization of Soviet agriculture and the creation of Gosagroprom. Both in the original decree establishing Gosagroprom and in the statute spelling out its structure, functions and responsibilities, the brief references to private farming appear almost as an afterthought.

In assessing the position of Gosagroprom within the administrative hierarchy in general, and the ministerial bureaucracy in particular, it is important to recognize that the new state agency has been given some special prerogatives and evidently far-flung functions and responsibilities. On the other hand, while its status—in terms of the legal provisions—is clearly superior to that of an ordinary ministry or state committee, a good deal of its proposed activity, according to its statute, is to take place "in accordance with established procedure." Moreover, at the end of the lengthy enumeration of the many functions of Gosagroprom, the statute states that, "in the execution, by the USSR State Agroindustrial Committee, of other functions connected with the activity of the gosagroproms of the union and autonomous republics, and the agroindustrial committees of the *krais* and *oblasts* and the administratively subordinated associations, enterprises, institutions and organizations in the sphere of planning, science and technology, capital construction, material-technical supply, finances and credit, personnel, labor and wages, as well as in the sphere of economic, scientific-technical, and cultural relations with foreign countries, it is guided by the General Statute on USSR Ministries."[24]

According to its statute, Gosagroprom, as a state committee, meets as necessary, but at least twice a year and examines the most important problems of the development of the agroindustrial complex of the country. The statute further provides that decisions taken by the collegium of the USSR State Agroindustrial Committee are put into effect, as a rule, through decrees and orders of the USSR Gosagroprom. In the case of disagreements between the Chairman of Gosagroprom and the collegium, the Chairman puts his decision into effect, reporting to the USSR Council of Ministers about the differences that have arisen, and members of the collegium, in their turn, may communicate their views to the USSR Council of Ministers.[25]

Gosagroprom: A Radical Reform or Another Step on the Treadmill?

The "restructuring" of agriculture may very well be the preferred pattern of Gorbachev for reorganization elsewhere in the Soviet economy, but thus far no other sectors of the Soviet economy have been similarly restructured. To date, coordination bodies—to be specific: bureaus in the USSR Council of Ministers—have been created for only two other sectors: The machine-building industries (in October 1985) and the fuel-energy complex (in March 1986). But the establishment of the Bureau for Machine Building and the Bureau for the Fuel-Energy Complex, unlike the establishment of Gosagroprom, did not involve the abolition of any of the much-maligned branch ministries; rather it involved the creation of yet another administrative layer above the ministries for which the two bureaus are responsible.

Thus, it would seem, Gosagroprom is the only real superministry to date which the Gorbachev administration has been able to create. It may well be that the Bureau for Machine Building and the Bureau for the Fuel-Energy Complex are the product of political compromise and do not actually represent Gorbachev's preferred solution to the problem of industrial reorganization. Be that as it may, the general thrust of what Gorbachev is trying to do is clear, i.e., to establish a small number of high-level organizations to supervise large, interrelated sectors of the Soviet economy and to concentrate on "the strategic heights" of planning and management—in short, to create a small number of relatively large complexes in such areas as agroindustry, fuel and energy, machine building, transportation, etc.

In assessing the meaning and significance of the establishment of Gosagroprom, it is important to recall that the idea of superministries is by no means new. On the contrary, for many years it has been part of Soviet official thinking concerning how to run the Soviet economy more efficiently. The idea of the creation of superministries, moreover, has figured prominently in the thinking of reform advocates in the Soviet academic community, some of whom have been in a position to offer policy advice to the Gorbachev administration. According to Boris Meissner, a proposal to streamline economic management by bringing "homogeneous and interrelated branches" together in complexes was entertained at the 25th CPSU Congress in 1976. However, nothing came of this proposal—evidently because Brezhnev and Kosygin did not see eye to eye on the subject of economic reform, or because the Presidium of the USSR Council of Ministers, which was charged with drawing up concrete reorganization proposals along this line in time for the 26th CPSU Congress, dragged its feet and failed to do so—perceiving correctly, no doubt, that the implementation of this idea would lead to a reduction in the power of the ministerial bureaucracy.[26]

Among academic specialists, the idea of consolidating branch ministries into a small number of complexes—based either on the consolidation of branch ministries with very similar functions (e.g., different types of transportation) or especially close relations between suppliers and customers (e.g., agriculture, agricultural machinery, and food processing)—can be associated with Professor K. K. Val'tukh, head of the Department for Rates of Social Production of the Institute of Economics and Organization of Industrial Production (IEOPP) in Novosibirsk University,[27] and B. P. Kurashvili, sector chief at the Institute of State and Law of the USSR Academy of Sciences in Moscow.[28] Finally, the branch ministries (and the phenomenon of "departmentalism" associated with them) were the target of particularly sharp criticism in the well-known Novosibirsk Report of Academician T. I. Zaslavskaia, which was presented to a group of high-level officials of Gosplan, the economics departments of the CPSU Central Committee, and the USSR Academy of Sciences.[29]

Of the new coordinating bodies that have been set up under Gorbachev, only Gosagroprom comes close to meeting the criticisms of the branch ministry system offered by academic specialists and officials in the Soviet Union. But while the new USSR State Agroindustrial Committee absorbed some of the functions of such agriculture-related ministries as the Ministry of Procurement (now the Ministry of Grain Products), the Ministry of Light Industry, and the Ministry of Land Improvement and Water Resources, these ministries were left outside the administrative authority of Gosagroprom—as were the Ministry of Tractor and Agricultural Machinery Production and the Ministry of Mineral Fertilizer Production. Thus, Gosagroprom, at least in its initial configuration, does not represent and encompass the "agroindustrial complex" in its entirety, at least not as it is (and ought to be) defined for planning purposes; neither does it control the important related branch ministries that supply the "complex" with such crucial inputs as mineral fertilizer and farm machinery.

Since the formation of Gosagroprom in 1985, a good deal has happened on the "organizational front" in Soviet agriculture. Within a few months after its establishment, Gosagroprom developed a "Model Statute of the Raion Agroindustrial Association"[30] and a "Model Statute of the State Agroindustrial Committee of the Autonomous Republic and the Agroindustrial Committee of the *Krai* and *Oblast.*"[31] Recommendations for wages of *sovkhoz* and *kolkhoz* workers from gross income were approved by Gosagroprom and the USSR State Committee for Labor and Social Problems and coordinated with the All-Union Central Trade Union Council.[32] A number of progress reports on the reorganization in various union republics have been published in *Eko-nomika sel'skogo khoziaistva,* the organ of Gosagroprom.[33] Already in June, 1986, this journal claimed that "now the organizational restructuring of the management of the agroindustrial complex has basically been completed at all levels."[34] Subdivisions for the agroindustrial complex have been created in the USSR Ministry of France, Gosplan, and the USSR State Committee for Science and Technology, but not yet in the USSR State Committee for Material and Technical Supply, Gosbank, the USSR State Committee for Labor and Social Problems, the USSR State Committee on Prices, and the USSR Central Statistical Administration.

There is little question that the establishment of Gosagroprom entailed traumatic personnel changes among the officialdom formerly in charge of agriculture. According to V. S. Murakhovskii, the chairman of Gosagroprom, 47 percent of the former staff of the ministries absorbed into Gosagroprom were removed from the central management apparatus for agriculture.[35] Some 3,200 officials were dismissed from their positions and had to be employed elsewhere.[36] One of the short-run effects of the reorganization in agriculture, therefore, was rather dramatic personnel change and a very significant reduction of the central management staff. However, only time will tell whether these effects will last and become a permanent feature in the physiognomy and evolution of Soviet agriculture. Given the past record of Soviet hierarchical reorganization, it is entirely possible (and, some would argue, even likely) that we will see a recreation of the abolished ministries and state committee in the guise of internal subdivisions of an expanded Gosagroprom.

Most of the problems in Soviet agriculture, it can be argued, can be attributed to excessive centralization in the planning, control and management of agriculture, irrational and inappropriate price policies, and flawed and ineffective incentive systems for farm managers, farm workers, and management personnel and workers of enterprises that supply the various inputs to agriculture and process, transport and market agricultural products. The reorganization of Soviet agriculture in the form of the establishment of Gosagroprom in itself will not cure these problems. As a matter of fact, it may be argued that the November 23, 1985 *perestroika* in Soviet agriculture was a step in the direction of greater centralization. Much will depend on whether the farms and various agriculture-related enterprises and industries will actually be granted significantly greater and meaningful autonomy in the long run. Furthermore, it remains to be seen to what extent Gosagroprom will be able to resist the temptation to intervene in micro-management affairs in the case of enterprises and associations, state and collective farms, which are not performing to expectation, but for whose performance Gosagroprom is responsible. All in all, it would seem that the steps taken by Gorbachev in agriculture in terms of hierarchical organization thus far suggest a rather conservative stance—the stance of a political leader who remains firmly convinced of the inherent viability of the Soviet model of socialism, the necessity and desirability of central planning, and the possibility of solving deeply-rooted economic problems through personnel and hierarchical change. As a matter of fact, it may be argued that Gorbachev remains convinced of the basic soundness of the premises underlying the 1965 reforms and is desperately trying to make them work through the appropriate mobilization measures, the anti-alcohol and discipline campaigns. . . . In that sense, we may be justified in concluding that, for the time being at least, Gosagroprom is best seen as another step on the treadmill, not as a radical reform. In the short run, however, there is little question that Gosagroprom's future and Gorbachev's political position have received a strong boost by the impressive performance of Soviet agriculture in 1986, the year following the reorganization. Due to a good grain crop and a considerable improvement in the performance of the livestock sector, Soviet agriculture rebounded from its poor performance in 1984 and 1985, registering a healthy 7.3 percent growth and helping to bolster the growth of Soviet GNP to over 4 percent, the highest in nearly a decade.[37]

Notes

1. A Bureau for Machine Building was set up approximately a month before the establishment of Gosagroprom. (See *Pravda*, October 22, 1985.) It was probably modeled on the Military-Industrial Commission (VKP), which coordinates the work of defense-related industries. Unlike Gosagroprom, however, this bureau did not replace existing ministries, but instead is interposed as an additional administrative layer between the ministries and the Council of Ministries, of which it is a part.

2. T. I. Zaslavskaia is a full member of the USSR Academy of Sciences and holds a number of prominent academic positions, including president of the Soviet Sociological Association. Boris Kurashvili is a section chief in the Institute of State and Law of the USSR Academy of Sciences in Moscow.

3. See my paper "Soviet Agriculture as the Touchstone of Economic Reform," presented at the Second International Congress of Professors World Peace Academy,

Hotel Intercontinental, Geneva, Switzerland, August 13–18, 1985, to be published in M. A. Kaplan and A. Shtromas, eds., *Russia's Crisis and Future*, Vol. II (New York: Paragon House and Macmillan, forthcoming).

4. See *Izvestiia*, June 1, 1985, p. 2.

5. For a summary of the decree establishing Gosagroprom, see *Pravda*, November 23, 1985, pp. 1–2.

6. See the decree of the Presidium of the USSR Supreme Soviet, *Pravda*, November 23, 1985, p. 2.

7. *Pravda*, November 23, 1985, p. 1.

8. See *Radio Liberty Research Bulletin*, RL 19/1985, January 21, 1985. For a discussion of the particular problems of this ministry, see *Ekonomika stroitel'stva*, No. 11, 1984.

9. For the statute of Gosagroprom, see "Polozhenie o Gosudarstvennom agropromyshlennom komitete SSSR," *Ekonomika sel'skogo khoziaistva*, No. 9, 1986, pp. 86–95.

10. This ministry was originally established in 1953 from parts of the Ministry of Agriculture. In 1969 it was renamed the Ministry of Procurement (*Minzag*). In December 1985, finally, the designation of this ministry changed once again to Ministry of Grain Products.

11. See "Polozhenie . . . ," pp. 94–95.

12. *Ibid.*

13. *Ibid.*

14. See Central Intelligence Agency, Directorate of Intelligence, *Directory of Soviet Officials: National Organizations* (Washington, D.C.: 1986), pp. 156–57; and *Directory of Soviet Officials: National Organizations* (Washington, D.C.: 1987), p. 156.

15. See "Polozhenie . . . ," pp. 94–95.

16. *Ibid.*, p. 95.

17. *Ibid.*, pp. 86–87. Citation from p. 87.

18. *Ibid.*, pp. 88–94.

19. *Ibid.*, p. 89.

20. *Ibid.*, p. 93.

21. *Ibid.*

22. *Pravda*, November 23, 1985, p. 2.

23. See "Polozhenie . . . ," p. 93.

24. *Ibid.*, p. 94.

25. *Ibid.*, pp. 94–95.

26. See Boris Meissner, "The 26th Party Congress and Soviet Domestic Politics," *Problems of Communism*, vol. 30, no. 3 (May-June 1981): 13.

27. K. K. Val'tukh, "Intensifikatsiia i sovershenstvovanie upravleniia," *EKO*, no. 2 (1977): 4–26.

28. See B. P. Kurashvili, "Sud'by otraslevogo upravleniia," EKO, no. 10 (1983): 34–55, and "Kontury vozmozhnogo perestroiki," *EKO*, no. 5 (1985): 59–79.

29. See Philip Hanson, "The Novosibirsk Report," *Survey*, Spring 1984, pp. 83–87; for the text of the report, see *ibid.*, pp. 88–108.

30. "Tipovoe polozhenie o raionnom agropromyshlennom ob"edinenii," *Ekonomika sel'skogo khoziaistva*, no. 7 (1986): 86–95.

31. "Tipovoe polozhenie o gosudarstvennom agropromyshlennom komitete avtonomnoi respubliki, agropromyshlennom komitete kraia, oblasti," in *Ekonomika sel'skogo khoziaistva*, no. 8 (1986): 86–94.

32. "Rekomendatsii po oplate truda rabotnikov sokhozov i kolkhoznikov ot valogo dokhoda," *Ekonomika sel'skogo khoziaistva*, no. 11 (1986): 87–95.

33. See the relevant articles in *Ekonomika sel'skogo khoziaistva* on the Kazakh SSR SSR (No. 9, 1986, pp. 27–32), the Azerbaijan SSR (No. 9, 1986, pp. 32–39), the Ukrainian SSR (No. 11, 1986, pp. 10–23), the Turkmen SSR (No. 12, pp. 23–27), and the Armenian SSR (No. 12, pp. 16–22).

34. See "Sovershenstvovat' khoziaistvennyi mekhanizm v APK," in *Ekonomika sel'skogo khoziaistva*, no. 6 (1986): 12.

35. See *Literaturnaia gazeta*, February 21, 1986, p. 2.

36. See *Sel'skaia zhizn'*, February 21, 1986 (account of press conference).

37. For an assessment of the Soviet economy under Gorbachev, see "Gorbachev's Modernization Program: A Status Report." Paper presented by the Central Intelligence Agency and the Defense Intelligence Agency for Submission to the Subcommittee on National Security Economics of the Joint Committee, Congress of the United States, March 19, 1987, to be published in Congress of the United States, Joint Economic Committee, "Allocation of Resources in the Soviet Union and China," Part 12, 1987.

David A. Dyker

Restructuring and "Radical Reform" The Articulation of Investment Demand

I. Introduction: Investment Policy and Investment Strategy

In the central part of this paper I will be looking at how producing units in the Soviet economy (enterprises, production associations) and inter-mediate planning bodies (ministries and formerly industrial associ-ations) articulate investment programs and apply pressure for their implementation.[1] I will produce evidence to suggest that these execu-tive bodies must bear a large proportion of the immediate responsibil-ity for the excess demand for investment resources that is such a dominant feature of the Soviet economic scene, and for specific distor-tions of resource allocation present in the investment process. I shall go on to look at Gorbachev's specific proposals aimed at altering the situation. But the Soviet economy is still a centrally planned economy, or at least it is meant to be, and Mr. Gorbachev surely intends it to continue like that. Accordingly, we must start by looking at how the *central* authorities generate investment demand, directly and indirectly. This involves assessing three dimensions of policy-making: develop-ment strategy, the rules of the game, and the appraisal of individual projects. Let us look at these in turn.

Sectoral priorities and centralization apart, the most important as-pect of traditional Soviet development strategy in relation to the invest-ment sphere is taut planning through material balances. In pursuing a policy of crude growth maximization, the Soviet planners have in the past sought to maintain maximum pressure on producing units by setting ambitious, sometimes improbably ambitious output targets,

---

The author teaches at the University of Sussex.

trusting that the resultant gaps in material balances would be made up in the short run through extra effort or good luck, or ultimately by the application of a draconian priority principle that recognized true worth only in heavy industry. Since the 1960s Soviet planners have sometimes threatened to make the transition to "slack" planning. But the stresses imposed by falling growth rates have tended to block this transition, and since the death of Brezhnev the talk has been all about raising the norms, toughening-up on discipline, etc.—slogans hardly compatible with a more relaxed attitude towards pressure in planning. As we shall see later on, this movement back towards tauter planning has been concretized in the form of explicit plan targets in the Gorbachev era. The trend is of particular importance in the present context because a number of the more idiosyncratic specific features of the investment process in the Soviet Union flow directly from the history of taut planning.

Why has that process been so insensitive to cost and lead-time parameters? Because Stalin was a good Marxist and thought that capital goods were free? We should certainly not dismiss the pure ideological dimension altogether. Nevertheless Soviet planners had already in the early 1930s developed an early version of the Coefficient of Relative Effectiveness (CRE), a substitute rate of interest, suggesting that there was no real problem of principle preventing a functional assessment of investment costs. I would argue that the nub of the matter has rather been the way that the interaction of taut planning and material balances has impinged on the investment sphere. Taut planning aims to foster creative tension through bottlenecks. If we follow Charles Wilber's argument,[2] we can say that it also aims to generate signals to investment planners—a hole in the plan means that it is time to build some new capacity somewhere. But because the material balances technique does not go beyond the level of crude general equilibrium analysis, because it is devoid of a resource allocation dimension, it gives these signals in a misleadingly absolute form, without reference to possible trade-offs, intersectorally, intertemporally, or whatever. The CRE was, of course, developed as a way of assessing the relative merits of different technological bases for making a given addition to production capacity. At least some Soviet economists were, one should add, already deeply aware of this weakness of the material balances method in the prewar period. Thus B. Sukharevskii was complaining as early as 1937 that investment plans were being elaborated "not from the angle of establishing proportions of increased reproduction but from the angle of centralized rationed supply of these types of product and of meeting the needs of first priority consumers.''[3] To underline just how resistant to treatment this syndrome is in the planned economies of Eastern Europe, let me quote Paul Hare, writing in 1983: ''Central agencies also persisted in undertaking projects seen as 'necessary' given economic balances prepared in quantity terms. The outcome was the persistence of investment cycles quite similar in form to those that arose before the reforms, creating serious difficulties for macroeconomic demand management.''[4] Hare was, of course, writing not about the Soviet Union, but about Hungary under the New Economic Mechanism.

We should, certainly, always bear the historical context of these characteristics firmly in mind. Soviet investment planning has been carried on in an essentially autonomous way, with the emphasis very much on ''assimilation,'' and with little regard for the capital-output ratio—$\Delta K/\Delta Y$—has simply not been an important planning indicator. This reflects the development of Soviet-type planning as having a mobilizing impetus, with capital investment—machines and buildings—playing a key role in helping to mobilize the ''abundant'' resources of labor, land, energy, and raw materials. It is as the supply of resources has tended to dry up that the weaknesses of this approach to investment planning have come to the fore. One of the ways the Soviet authorities have reacted to the problem of changing gears is to put a special premium on ''reconstruction and technical reequipment''— i.e., retooling and upgrading—of existing enterprise production capacities, as a way of reducing the historically high buildings component in Soviet investment, and encouraging swifter completion and a higher rate of technical progress. This, indeed, is the background to many of the specifically investment-oriented policy initiatives of the Andropov-Gorbachev period.

Such strategic considerations have impinged strongly on the evolution of the rules of the game, as formulated by the central authorities. Every investment undertaking in the Soviet Union must have a ''title list'' (*titul'nyi spisok*), a document of about six pages detailing the main technical characteristics of the project.[5] Up until 1979 these included no breakdowns of construction by year. It was only in 1981, with the publication of a new official investment-appraisal methodology, that design organizations were for the first time charged with checking their prognostications about investment ''effectiveness'' against actual outcomes.[6] The 1981 methodology was also the first official document to specify a set of norms for absolute or general economic effectiveness, calculated in terms of the relationship between streams of national income and investment—the inverse of the incremental capital-output ratio. But none of these are revolutionary changes—the Coefficient of Absolute Effectiveness is so couched mathematically as to be of little operational value[7] —and their introduction rather serves merely to highlight the depth of specific lacunae in the traditional panoply of Soviet investment planning.

It is only in the case of "the most important projects" (formerly defined as those worth more than 150 million rubles) that the actual detailed design has to be approved by the central authorities. Beyond that, "above-limit" centralized investment has been controlled—if that is the right word—by the center through the title list. Projects worth less than three million rubles have traditionally come into the category of "below-limit" centralized investment, and block votes have been given to ministries and republican governments to finance such projects, with those intermediate bodies taking over the job of approving title lists or determining who does. Thus small-to-medium "centralized" investment projects have been firmly under the control of intermediate planning bodies, with few guidelines, never mind instructions, from the center to "help" them. Enterprises and associations have always been permitted to accumulate "production development funds," in principle autonomous, to finance some retooling and upgrading investment under the rubric of "decentralized investment." Decentralized investment was much featured in the Kosygin planning reform, and by 1972 it accounted for nearly 20 percent of total state investment.[8] But this initiative fell afoul of the reaction of the late-Brezhnev period, and by the middle 1970s decentralized investment had to all intents and purposes been absorbed into the centralized category, with ministries shifting funds around and deciding on projects.[9] The 1979 planning decree intimated some movement back towards an autonomous status for decentralized investment, but it was only with the introduction of Andropov's industrial planning experiment, and subsequently of the Sumy/VAZ experiment, that decentralized investment began to take on key operational importance. Historically, it is probably more realistic to see the role and power of the producing unit in the Soviet investment process in terms of that unit's monopoly over much crucial information, rather than in terms of formal powers of disposal over substantial blocks of investment funds.

To complete the picture we have to say something about modes of finance. One of the key characteristics of the classical Stalinist system is the nonreturnable budgetary grant as the financial basis for the great bulk of state investment, and this characteristic underwent little change through the period before 1965. Kosygin's planning reform of that year put a new emphasis on retained profits as a source of finance for centralized investment, and by 1972 retained profits accounted for 60 percent of total finance for centralized investment in industry, with budgetary grants covering just 33.8 percent.[10] This made no formal difference to the incidence of decision-making power, but it must surely have increased enterprise directors' effective say in centralized investment matters, to the extent that they had independent control over the profit parameter. It was also a principle of the 1965 reform that bank credit should become an important source of investment finance. This never happened, and in 1974 bank credit accounted for only 7.68 percent of total industrial centralized investment finance.[11] Quite apart from the question of who articulates investment demands, this underlines what is perhaps the most important feature of the whole traditional investment set-up for present purposes. Investment grants from the center are obviously free to the ministry or enterprise. In a situation where gross profit margins are high and protected by administratively fixed prices, and where there is no opportunity cost in terms of investments foregone outside the enterprise, investment finance coming from retained profits is nearly as free. We will have to bear this very firmly in mind when we come to consider Gorbachev's investment reforms. Staying with the pre-reform system for the moment, we should finally note that while some ministries have reported very high rates of self-financing since the late 1960s, none borrow for investment purposes. Thus for the main instance of fixed capital formation decision-taking outside the sphere of the central planners investment remained basically a free good. This is obviously of tremendous importance in the analysis of excess demand for investment resources.

As we saw, the center involves itself in the text of actual designs only for very big projects. But that does mean, for example, that the operational details of projects like the Kama Truck Factory, the BAM, and the big East-West pipelines, are directly overseen by the center. To the extent that it is these priority projects that determine the profile of development of the Soviet economy, and to the extent that they generate some of the pressures that maintain a degree of tautness in that economy, then we must be prepared to see the center as a source of specific, microeconomic investment demands with important spillover effects. Coming back again to excess investment demand, the center may in principle be as guilty as anybody of getting too many projects going at a given time. We shall return to this point later.

The Profile of Investment Demand

Excessive lead-times—two or three times as long as in the West—reflect a complex of factors in the Soviet economy, including operational inefficiencies at the level of design and construction organizations and erratic supply of building materials and equipment. But there cannot be the slightest doubt that excess demand for investment has been a major, perhaps the major, factor involved. S. Bulgakov estimated in 1984 that normed lead-times could be achieved in the Soviet Union only at the cost of abandoning half the projects then under construction.[12] If we take at face value the endless government campaigns to reduce the number of projects simultaneously under construction, then we should exclude the center from culpability on this count. I am not sure that we should, but it is certainly much easier to pinpoint the guilt of lower bodies. Thus for instance ministries have in the past been notorious for starting projects not actually in the plan.[13] They have frequently stood accused of fiddling the initial estimates on projects, just to keep them below the "limit" and keep the center out of the approval process. That was why, for example, the Ministry for Ferrous Metallurgy pushed through a 6-million-ruble project in Kemerevo as a 2.5-million-ruble project,[14] thus implicitly bagging large volumes of resources earmarked for other projects. We have demonstrated that investment resources are virtually a free good to the ministry or enterprise under "unrestructured" Soviet conditions, which explains why executive bodies have been able to overbid for investment resources with impunity. It does not explain why they have felt themselves to be under such pressure to take maximum advantage of that impunity. To make a cross-systemic comparison, the early and middle 1970s were characterized in the U.K. by sharply negative real rates of interest and a government philosophy that took readily to bailing-out operations for firms that had got themselves into trouble with investment ventures. Throughout the period Great Britain continued to report the lowest investment ratio among the industrial countries of Europe. What is special about the Soviet context is the way that the specific environment in which executive bodies work has interacted with the general environment imposed by the strategic choices of the central authorities. Let us try to put more flesh onto this general proposition by listing the proximate factors that put pressure on ministries and enterprises to overbid for investment resources, viz.:

(1) In a bureaucratic set-up, the more projects you manage to start in period 1, the easier it is to obtain additional investment funds in period 2. That is why ministries have been so prone to starting projects not in the plan.

(2) Going one step further, there is a marked reluctance to abandon projects once started, because the existing resource shares exert a considerable influence on future allocations.[15] Any writing-off therefore weakens a negotiator's position.

(3) Where supply uncertainty is endemic, clients may wish to have as many projects as possible on the go, simply in order to be sure of always having something they can be getting on with.

(4) To the extent that enterprises are permitted to accumulate production development funds for decentralized investment, they may feel anxious to spend these accumulations as quickly as possible, a) in case a future change of policy results in partial or total confiscation; b) to reduce the possibility of such a change occurring, by demonstrating that they are capable of using the funds. The volatility of policy on decentralized investment over the last 20 years must have fortified any tendency on the part of Soviet managers to take a very short view in this matter.

Points 1, 2, and 4 parallel the experience of any executive who has had to try to guarantee resource flows from a centralized bureaucracy. Point 3 confirms how centralization and taut planning can, through the medium of supply uncertainty, exacerbate what might be called the pure negotiating factors. The way that executive bodies react to supply uncertainty may have more far-reaching effects on specific *allocational* patterns in investment.

We should, certainly, avoid the temptation to place exclusive emphasis on executive body reaction when we look at resource allocation patterns in the process of articulation of executive-body demand for investment. The best way to illustrate this is by citing Boris Rumer's research on Brezhnev's retooling and upgrading initiative.[16] Why did this policy not achieve its stated aim of raising the rate of technical progress at the factory-floor level? Because in practice managers used the rubric as a pretext for obtaining new, non-innovative equipment, in the process often scrapping equipment that had not been fully amortized. They did this because they felt obliged to make some response to the government campaign, since otherwise they might have fallen under suspicion of lack of commitment, or at any rate missed out on their share of a big cake. But the easiest response is a simulated one, particularly since changes in production technology always threaten the rhythm of output plan fulfillment, so that calls for greater technological dynamism tend to produce a diametrically opposite result. The resultant resource misallocation is palpable. What is less clear is whom we should blame for this. If we are trying to pinpoint the initiators of investment demand, then we should perhaps in this case focus on the central authorities. It was, after all, they who were demanding something called "reconstruction and technical re-equipment," and the consequent difficulties arose, as so often in centralized systems, because they were unable in practice to be sufficiently precise about what they meant by that rubric. Whether Gorbachev's reprise of the reconstruction and re-equipment initiative promises better results is a key question we shall address in due course.

But when we turn to misallocations that result from distortions of *production profile*, we are firmly in the province of demands initiated by ministries and enterprises. The tendency to organizational autarky in the Soviet Union has been so thoroughly researched that in the present context there is no need to do more than sum up. Faced with chronic supply uncertainty, executive bodies adopt a do-it-yourself policy. Ministries use small enterprises, often in peripheral areas, to produce accessories and semi-finisheds. Enterprises use "dwarf-workshops" to do the same thing on a smaller scale. The below-limit and decentralized investment categories have provided plenty of financial scope for this kind of thing, and a good deal of simulated upgrading investment may be oriented towards safeguarding supplies. Going one step further, the pressure on enterprises to get rid of perfectly serviceable equipment ensures that clients can often avoid the official material supply network in procuring the machines they need. Thus locational patterns and capital-labor ratios have been distorted and excess capacity built into the structure of the economy, with executive bodies hanging onto small production units just in case. As the central authorities have endeavored in recent years to reorient the planning system towards solution of the key problem of labor shortage, so the tendency to organizational autarky has emerged as a major obstacle to rationalization schemes. Under the Shchekino system, first introduced in 1967, managers were allowed to create redundancies, and use some of the money thus saved to pay higher wages to the remaining workers. This system was originally developed in the chemicals industry and has been successfully generalized in that sector, dominated as it is by fairly straightforward, linear production-line technology. But attempts to extend it into the engineering industry were much less successful.[17] Quite simply, engineering directors have not been prepared to give up their all-purpose production profiles, because they would rather make their own nuts and bolts than trust another to supply them. Not surprisingly, then, labor productivity in the Soviet engineering industry remains low by international standards. Nor is it surprising that Mr. Gorbachev has been intent on widening application of the Shchekino principle under the rubric of his planning experiments.

What about regional authorities? It is republican governments that allocate below-limit investment votes for infrastructural investment, sometimes decentralizing the approval process further down to the provincial level. Soviet industrial ministries have been notoriously neglectful of infrastructural investment, understandably, perhaps, given the pressures they are under to deliver the goods in terms of short-term output performance. As a result, most of the stories we hear about battles over infrastructural allocations have the ministries firmly in the role of the baddies, and local government and local Party committees in that of the goodies. We should, of course, be skeptical of the notion that local political authorities are always on the side of the allocational angels. Like all political structures, they evince a weakness for prestige projects—during the *sovnarkhoz* period (1957–65), when local bodies took over the role of the industrial ministries, there was a rash of localism too severe to be explained wholly by rational response to supply problems.[18] The late-Brezhnev period witnessed some movement in the direction of more power to the elbow of local authorities in investment matters, including production investment matters, and more recent reports suggest that the Gorbachev leadership would like to see this trend continue. Thus for example the Bashkiriia *obkom,* working through Stroibank, succeeded in cutting out 200 million rubles' worth of ''unnecessary'' projected investments in 1984.

For instance the Ministry for the Chemicals Industry had planned construction of a number of new plants at the Kaustik association in Sterlitamak. When the Party obkom looked at this question doubts were raised about whether the plants were needed, particularly inasmuch as they intended to use equipment that could not be considered satisfactory. Specialists, including Stroibank specialists, were instructed to make a detailed study of the matter. From this it transpired that the technology recommended to Kaustik was obsolete, and that attempts to introduce it elsewhere in the Soviet Union have been unsuccessful. Naturally, the project was vetoed.[19]

Here the local political establishment is cast in the role of guardian of technological dynamism. Of course local politicians also like to see output targets fulfilled, so we should be careful about generalizing from cases like these. Nevertheless regional and local political authorities do introduce some corrective to the penchants of production organizations, and must be reckoned with in any survey of the initiators of investment demand.

III. Economic Reform and Investment Demand

Continuing with the (naive) assumption that the central authorities would dearly and unreservedly like to expunge all these "imperfections" from the investment demand profile, let us now look at the policy departures that have touched on the problem in recent years. In 1982 Gosplan decided to create a Unified System of Planning for Capital Investment—ESPKS (*Edinaia sistema planirovaniia kapital'-nogo stroitel'stva*), founded on a computerized information base containing "all design and title list indicators, and all related norms."[20] Work on the creation of this system was not scheduled to finish until January 1, 1986, and was in fact still dragging on in mid-1986.[21] Nevertheless when the first comprehensive decree on the investment system for a long time was published in June 1984,[22] at a time when Gorbachev was already in control of economic policy-making, it seemed to show a new confidence in the ability of the center to put its investment house in order. The main elements in the decree were as follows:

(1) Planned levels of investment were to be balanced with plans for investment finance, supply of building materials and equipment for installation, and the production capacity of the building industry. In other words, supply was to equal demand in every conceivable direction, which would seem to exclude any elements of taut planning. If we can swallow the latter point, we must certainly be skeptical about the capacity of ESPKS to revolutionize the plan-consistency situation to any dramatic extent, in what remains a grossly overcentralized system. As we know, Soviet computers are technically backward, and Soviet central planning has a surprisingly poor record on rational utilization of computer networks. ESPKS was clearly meant to represent an attack on

that problem: yet we find that the system was not to be independent of the existing administrative structure of the Soviet economy. On the contrary, it was to operate through the hierarchy of Gosplan USSR, republican Gosplans, and industrial ministries, with information on below-limit projects stored at republican and ministerial levels. But in the blunt words of Academician Fedorenko, "the main obstacle to the assimilation of mathematical-economic models and methods is present-ed by deficiencies in the economic mechanism."[23] More specifically in relation to the matter under consideration, "the successful formulation of balanced plans at the central level [through ESPKS—D.A.D.] re-quires a corresponding improvement in the technology of planning at the lower levels."[24] Fedorenko went on to argue that as long as mathe-matical-economic methods help ministries and enterprises to fulfill given plans, managers welcome them. As soon as they are used to help work out the plans, to "uncover hidden reserves," the attitude changes. He cites a number of cases where industrial ministries have indeed obstructed or terminated ASU (automatic control systems) re-search programs relating to production potential in their sectors. Now overbidding for investment funds, organizational autarky, etc., are all about the "safety factor," all about how working organizations cope with the vagaries of the system. And here we can pinpoint a paradox that neatly sums up the whole dilemma of Soviet planning. ESPKS had to be decentralized because of the weight of the burden of centralized planning on Gosplan and its allied institutions. But precisely because the system as a whole, and in particular the supply system, remained so overcentralized, inflexible, and clumsy, executive bodies would inevi-tably continue to be dominated by short-term survival considerations. That is why the ministries were quite unfit to be trusted with the development of ESPKS.

It is unclear exactly what has been the impact on ESPKS of Gorba-chev's reforms, with their penchant for taking functions away from the ministries. In principle we would expect that the more the intermediate executive body was freed of the obligation to supervise plan fulfill-ment, the better able it would be to serve strictly informational pur-poses. It is my impression, however, that the relocation further down the hierarchy of specific elements of investment decision-taking has *not* meant any dilution of ministerial responsibility of *aggregate* perfor-mance.

(2) By January 1, 1985, all design and estimate documentation for projects carrying over to the next five-year plan was to be reviewed

with a view to cutting out unnecessary elements, postponing projects of secondary importance, and ensuring that embodied technologies be up to date. The deadline was obviously quite unreal, but the initiative is worth assessing on its ongoing merits. It involved a number of supply-side issues, but let us concentrate on the demand side here. Once again, the work was to be entrusted to the ministries, and so all the things said about executive bodies in the last section can be repeated. To make matters worse, the whole dimension of valuation of construction projects has lately been in turmoil, following the introduction of a new system of estimate prices and norms on January 1, 1984. By April 1984 only 65 percent of estimates for projects due to be commissioned in that year had been revised,[25] and as of early 1987 there were still many gaps in the investment estimate norm system.[26] Now with all this revision of prices, how can ministries or any other bodies even know what they are doing as they try to respond to pressure to get estimates down? In line with the general tenor of economic policy, the onus for keeping down investment costs is now being shifted to the enterprise level, through the system, first tried out experimentally in Belorussia and Lithuania in 1982, whereby project prices are agreed on between client and contractor—on the basis of centrally determined norms. This approach was officially programmed for generalization in the decree on the planning of the construction complex published in October 1986.[27] But as Gosstroi (State Construction Committee) chairman Batalin has recently said, it will only work if the norms are right—see my initial point regarding the ministries—and if clients and contractors are given enough freedom of maneuver to give them a real interest in cost-cutting. This latter point brings up a number of fundamental issues to which I shall return later on. What is quite clear is that as of 1987 the attempt to cut back on excessive spread on the investment front had still not really bitten. Around that time, according to Batalin, the average lead-time in the Soviet Union was still eight or nine years.[28]

(3) Housing and amenities investments should be planned in strict conjunction with production investments, and should be commissioned when the latter are commissioned. Again, this seems rather ambitious. In a system that cannot guarantee balance between different parts of the plan, you need "soft" sectors to take the strain when things go wrong. The soft sectors have to be outside the main production cycle, for obvious reasons, and in the construction sphere that usually means infrastructural investment. Gorbachev has committed himself to changing this pattern, and Batalin again assures us that "a key characteristic

of the new investment policy is the movement away from the 'residual' approach to the allocation of resources for the needs of the social sphere.''[29] How feasible such a change-over is in the context of Gorbachev's general growth-and-development priorities is another matter.

(4) Feasibility studies (TEOs—*tekhniko-ekonomicheskie obosnovaniia*) were to be re-introduced as an independent element in project planning for large-scale and complicated projects. The history of feasibility studies in the Soviet Union is a painful one. Partly because design organizations have been badly underpaid for this kind of work, partly because ministries are not interested in locational rationality, except in their own departmentalist terms, TEOs have often been very poorly done, and this has had a serious and damaging effect on the quality of Soviet project assessment. In 1981 it was decided to abolish TEOs as such, and integrate their content into an upgraded system of sectoral and regional development and location schemes—under the respective aegis of ministries and regional governments. This did not work, so they have gone back to the old system—with the ministries initially in charge. The new system of estimate norms may make the design organizations happier to spend time on feasibility studies. It will not, however, affect the results of feasibility studies very much, if hierarchical pressures operate as powerfully in the future as they have in the past. ''To get construction started at any cost, and that means having to prove that the given project is economically highly attractive—that is in many cases the unspoken behest to the design worker.''[30] The key innovation in the revamped TEO system ties in directly with the contract price system, as discussed under (2), above. The idea now is that the contract price should be agreed upon between client and contractor on the basis of the TEO.[31] Thus if the contract price system generates the right pressures, the general quality of TEOs should certainly now rise.

The 1984 investment planning decree was in itself a disappointing document. It listed desiderata rather than solutions, and carried little analysis of the fundamental problems of the Soviet investment cycle. At the same time it did provide signposts to a number of Gorbachev's investment policy gambits. The most important of those gambits was the greatly increased role allotted to decentralized investment under Gorbachev's extension of the industrial-planning experiment originally set up by Andropov to run from January 1, 1984, and under the Sumy and VAZ experiments now programmed for extension to selected sectors from January 1, 1987.

Going far beyond Kosygin's measures of 1965, the Soviet planners are now saying that the great bulk of retooling and upgrading investments should come into the decentralized investment category, i.e., be planned by the enterprise and financed through the production development fund, either from retained profits or bank loans. The mid–1985 decree on the industrial planning experiment specified that retooling and upgrading investments financed from the production-development fund of an estimated value of up to 4 million rubles in heavy industry, and up to 2.5 million rubles elsewhere, should be planned independently by enterprises; above that value the plans are subject to examination (*rassmatrivat'*) by the relevant ministry.[32] What this means is that virtually all the investment that used to be in the below-limit centralized category, and even some of what used to be above-limit, will now be classed as decentralized. That is a body-blow to the ministries, and represents a major shift in the nexus of production investment decision-taking towards the enterprise and association. In addition, enterprise sociocultural and housing funds are being expanded under the rubric of the industrial-planning experiment, so that the focus of some types of infrastructural investment is also being shifted towards the producing unit. Mr. Batalin no doubt had this in mind when he spoke about getting away from the "residual approach" to infrastructural investment planning. With the generalization of the industrial-planning experiment throughout Soviet industry on January 1, 1987, these new principles passed beyond the experimental stage.

The Sumy/VAZ experiment simply brings the profit-plowback side of the industrial-planning experiment to its logical conclusion. Under "100 percent self-financing," enterprises are allowed to retain a high (under the original Sumy experiment 70 percent) and stable proportion of profits for their own uses, e.g., enterprise investment, infrastructural investment, and bonuses. While there is some scope for switching money between these three headings, the bulk of retentions should normally go into retooling, upgrading, and expansion investments. For the first time the whole of amortization funds would also be earmarked for this purpose, with the additional possibility of Stroibank credits. Thus under the Sumy/VAZ system responsibility for virtually all investment, apart from wholly new plants, passes to the enterprise or association.

We saw what a sad end Kosygin's decentralized investment policy came to in the mid–1970s. Are there substantial reasons for believing it will work better this time around? Let us start with technical difficulties. General political reaction apart, the reason why Brezhnev back-tracked on decentralized investment in the 1970s comes down to the supply difficulties would-be decentralized investors found themselves up against as soon as the reform provisions were promulgated. By introducing an autonomous element into investment planning and investment finance, but not into investment-supply planning, Kosygin and Brezhnev created a perverse bottleneck in the system. How can Gosplan and Gossnab plan supplies for projects that are by definition unknown to them? The answer is: they cannot. But they should not be trying to in the first place. It was because the Kosygin reform stopped short of introducing ''wholesale trade in the means of production'' that the deficiencies of bureaucratic materials allocation continued to plague the Soviet system. Specifically in the present context, enterprise managers found that they were not able to procure supplies to back up their decentralized investment plans through the official channels. They accordingly fled to the second economy, and by the early 1970s were very successfully filching supplies away from centralized investment projects—to such an extent as seriously to exacerbate the *raspylenie* problem on the investment scene as a whole at that time.[33] It is not surprising, perhaps, that conservative Communist Party cadres found this too much to swallow.

Exactly the same thing happened under the industrial planning experiment. Let us look at some early reports from enterprises put on the experiment from its inception. One director complained that with a production development fund of 1.2 million rubles in 1984, he was able to secure material supplies and equipment to the value of only 790,000 rubles. What would happen in 1985, when the fund was scheduled to grow to 1.6 million rubles?[34] Another pointed out that it was virtually impossible for small and medium-sized enterprises to get a construction organization to build houses for them—so what could they do with their enlarged sociocultural and housing funds?[35] A year or so on, we find the director of an engineering enterprise making exactly the same point, but with the difference that he suggests a solution to the problem—introduction of wholesale trade in the means of production.[36] Indeed by 1986, establishment Soviet economists were beginning to write off Andropov's experiment as having been excessively cautious and partial. Thus V. Moskalenko, the assistant general director of the Sumy association itself:

> The industrial planning experiment has made a significant contribution to the improvement of the economic mechanism. At the same time, however,

a number of problems have arisen, which is normal, in that with the solution of 'old' problems new ones arise. The main deficiency of the economic mechanism enshrined in the industrial-planning experiment lies in its failure to make a substantial impact on the problem of restructuring the system for financing capital investments and the development of production, and for introducing the achievements of science and technology at the enterprise level. But restructuring financing procedures, broadening autonomy, and increasing the level of responsibility of the enterprise in these areas are in fact the determining factors for fundamental improvement in other parts of the economic mechanism.[37]

We can go along with much of what Moskalenko says. But it is a little odd that he ends with the proposition that effective financial reform is a necessary condition for effective reform of the economic mechanism as a whole. Surely it is the other way around. Certainly we find the Sumy management complaining towards the end of 1985 about exactly the same problems of finding supplies for decentralized investment and housing construction as enterprises on the straight industrial planning experiment. Has anything changed in the meantime that is likely to give the Soviet supply system the flexibility it needs to respond to a more varied pattern of investment demand?

The signs are ambiguous. In a scholarly article published in 1986 Piotr Bunich stated that "nonplanned wholesale trade" is to be introduced for 10,000 user-enterprises in the course of 1987.[38] That could mean across-the-counter trading in substantial areas of investment supply. But Abel Aganbegyan, the most "official" of the academic economist voices, maintains, in his frequent public pronouncements, a studied vagueness on the possible role of the market mechanism within industry. You can, certainly, find unequivocal, radical points of view expressed in the Soviet press. Thus Academician A. Rumiantsev and Iu. Goland have argued in the pages of *Ekonomicheskaia gazeta* that "directive planning could be restricted to the production of just a narrow range of key products with stable demand. That means mainly fuel and energy resources, the most important types of raw materials, and custom-built pieces of equipment."[39] They go on to suggest that industrial enterprises should normally be allowed to devote part of their production capacity to the satisfaction of specific orders coming through the dimension of wholesale trade, with no planning targets as such involved at all. It is, they posit, "logical that the marketing of particular goods should be planned at the same level as their production." All of this would, of course, neatly solve the problem of supply to decentralized investment, though it would in the process change the

Soviet planning system beyond recognition. But the fact that such a view has been published in a Party newspaper may be more of a tribute to *glasnost'* than a sign of committed policy. What we can be quite sure of is that the more the nexus of investment demand is shifted towards the enterprise, the more serious, *ceteris paribus*, will investment supply problems at the micro level become. However radical Rumiantsev and Goland may sound, they are only working out the lateral implications of official policy.

That is not the end of complications with the self-financing approach. As we saw, there is every reason to expect, *a priori*, that managers flush with decentralized investment funds will want to spend them quickly, and the memory of what happened last time will spur them on in that. Thus we might expect the extent of aggregate overbidding for physical investment resources to increase, particularly where the existing price structure facilitates high ''normal'' rates of profit.

Most important of all is the shift in the focus of retooling and upgrading investment decision-taking likely to improve the allocation of resources? More specifically, is it likely to strengthen the innovation impetus that is supposed to reside in that category of investment? The July 1985 decree does expressly forbid ''simple replacement'' under the rubric of retooling and upgrading. But is prohibition backed up by appropriate planning measures? Clearly the more anxious enterprises are to spend all the production development fund as quickly as possible, the more they may be inclined to replace rather than innovate. To the extent that simulation of retooling and upgrading is intimately connected with the tyranny of the plan and the organizational autarky syndrome, and as long as Soviet enterprises, including those on the Sumy/ VAZ system, have supply uncertainty to cope with and output/sales targets to fulfill, cost/efficiency considerations will in any case continue to take second place for the enterprise. On the other hand, enterprise-level organizational autarky probably affords much less scope for simulated upgrading than ministry-level, inasmuch as it finds expression through dwarf-workshops and the like, which could hardly be passed off as technologically innovative. For the ministry, by contrast, renovation of the main production line of a subordinate enterprise may be precisely what is required to guarantee supplies to a sister enterprise, making the simulation in this case much harder to diagnose. We must nevertheless conclude that the *allocational* potential of the self-financing system is as dependent on the introduction of some flexibility in supply and pricing arrangements as any of its other dimensions.

On balance, then, the shift towards self-financing in investment embodied in the industrial planning experiment and the Sumy/VAZ experiment may tend to some improvement in resource-allocation patterns. But it could well intensify the problem of macro imbalance, in addition to exacerbating specific supply difficulties. Note that the more successful the experimental measures are in limiting the scope for organizational autarky, the less of an in-house safety factor will production organizations have to meet the ups and downs of the supply system, so that managers may find themselves forced more and more onto the gray market, to safeguard their general supply position. All roads, it seems, lead back to the issue of wholesale trade in the means of production.

IV. The Prospects for Effective Investment-Planning Reform

The easy lesson to read from all this is that the first thing the Russians must do is to introduce a significant dimension of market socialism. There can, indeed, be no quarrelling with that as a necessary condition for putting the investment house in order. But Yugoslavia and Hungary, the homelands of market socialism, have problems of *raspylenie* as serious as the Soviet Union, though there are virtually no supply-side reasons why it should be so.[40] This does, indeed, help us to isolate the ultimate causes of excess investment demand, and suggests that we should seek them in the realm of economic development strategy and general policy orientation rather than in specific features of planning systems. Perhaps the most telling body of evidence on this point comes from the period of the late 1920s in the Soviet Union, when the industrialization drive was beginning to get under way, though the edifice of Stalinist planning was not yet built. The extent of overbidding for investment resources seems to have been as powerful in this period as at any other time in Soviet history.[41]

Thus we find ourselves back with crude growth maximization, taut planning, and the extensive development model. Throughout the socialist world, from the Soviet Union through Poland to Albania and China, the notion has prevailed that in trying to overcome economic backwardness the higher you can get the investment ratio the better. Indeed before the Polish disaster there were a good many Western scholars, myself included, who had some sympathy with this idea. Historically it has reflected a view of investment as a primarily mobilizing factor, but in countries like Hungary that have been dominated by shortages of other things, particularly labor and raw materials, it has been transformed into a factor-substitution policy—not accompanied, unfortunately, by the necessary microeconomic adjustments.[42]

Translated to the sectoral and enterprise level, this means that the big spenders are always the favorite sons, the more so in that socialist governments have been more concerned than their capitalist counterparts to maximize employment and minimize unemployment. In the Yugoslav case, in which there is virtually no planning of investment as such at all, tautness is expressed through inflationary financing of almost everything, which produces negative real rates of interest and starts the investment ball rolling. The ball keeps rolling, and indeed gets out of control, because the authorities are much too ready to bail out bad investment choices, much too reluctant to enforce socialist bankruptcy.[43] One must add that in Hungary, where the investment process is still heavily bureaucratized, the problem is significantly worse. Nevertheless, the lesson for the Soviet Union is clear. It is tautness, in the specific operational form it takes in a Soviet-type economy, that makes the whole system so insensitive to return on investment. In the past ministries have continually started new projects outside the plan, not only because they knew they would not have to pay the bill, but also because they felt that the center never really disapproved. If we look at the check list of lead-times and cost escalations, we find that it is in any case the very big projects—the ones directly overseen by the central authorities—that have the worst record. Thus in the early 1970s, for example, the average cost escalation on five selected projects each worth more than 150 million rubles was almost 60 percent, while on a broad sample of 850 projects it was just 30 percent.[44] All those extra resources had to be bagged for the big sites, so that the Kremlin's own favorite projects must by themselves make a substantial contribution to the overall degree of overstrain on the investment front. In a period when Gorbachev has set the Soviet economy the task of gradually accelerating its rate of growth up to the end of the century, and specified new priorities particularly in the area of machine-building, as a principal vehicle for the implementation of that acceleration, we may just wonder whether the strategic environment is right for a fundamental rationalization of the investment scene.

When we come down to specific allocational problems the peculiarities of the Soviet planning system itself do impinge much more heavily. The perverse response to retooling and upgrading campaigns is purely a function of the way the bureaucratic game is played in the Soviet Union, and of the tyranny of short-term output targets. Organizational autarky is nothing more than a reflection of the supply problems caused by overcentralization, and its only connection with development strategy is that it was tolerable in the period of abundance of labor. If we accept the argument that labor productivity is now the most problematic area of the Soviet economy, then we must agree with the Soviet economists who see the tendency to organizational autarky as one of the most damaging features of contemporary Soviet industrial structure.[45] Here again, however, policy formulation is complicated by broader considerations. In the past Soviet leaders may have felt that dwarf-workshops did at least help to maintain full employment. Gorbachev has made it very clear that he puts efficiency above job security, and views the shaking-out of surplus labor as a key condition of acceleration. But while the Andropov/Gorbachev reforms have done much to facilitate work-force rationalization, they have done much less to establish a positive interest on the part of management in such rationalization. As long as the Soviet economy remains basically centrally planned, sensible Soviet directors will tend to hang onto surplus labor just in case.

The gist of these concluding observations is that the Soviet central authorities may be at best ambivalent in their ceaseless campaigning for better discipline in the investment field. A political scientist versed in the semiotic approach might take the argument further and suggest that the traditional devolution of much of the detail of investment planning to the ministries has provided the central authorities with a scapegoat always available to be blamed for all shortcomings, whatever their ultimate cause. The center, by contrast, escapes criticism because it continues to endorse and encourage things that, in very general terms, can only be described as "good."[46] Under the self-financing regime, enterprises and production associations might find themselves playing the same scapegoat role, especially if they have to break the rules to safeguard their investment-supply position.

I shall end by posing a series of connected questions that may help to clarify what are the necessary conditions for bringing order into the demand side of the investment process in the Soviet Union, viz.:

How much economic reform is required to break once and for all the Stalinist obsession with output to the detriment of efficiency and quality?

How serious do the problems have to become before the central authorities are prepared to give up their prerogative to adjust priorities, as and when they see fit?

Finally, when will the Soviet authorities permit planning experiments to proceed in such a way that responsibility for good or bad results can be attributed precisely, whether the finger points at some humble manager, or at the Kremlin itself?

Notes

1. This is a revised version of a paper presented to the III World Congress for Soviet and East European Studies, Washington, D.C., November 2, 1985.

2. C. K. Wilber, *The Soviet Model and Under-Developed Countries* (Chapel Hill: University of North Carolina Press, 1969), chapter V.

3. *Planovoe khoziaistvo*, nos. 11–12 (1937): 38, quoted in R. Hutchings, *The Structural Origins of Soviet Industrial Expansion* (London: Macmillan, 1984), p. 30.

4. P. Hare, "The Beginnings of Institutional Reform in Hungary," *Soviet Studies*, vol. 35, no. 3 (July 1983): 314.

5. Statement by V. Ivanov, in *Ekonomicheskaia gazeta*, no. 21, p. 9.

6. "Metodika opredeleniia ekonomicheskoi effektivnosti kapital'nykh vlozhenii," *Ekonomicheskaia gazeta*, nos. 2 & 3, 1981.

7. D. A. Dyker, *The Process of Investment in the Soviet Union* (Cambridge University Press, 1983), p. 108.

8. N. Baibakov, "O gosudarstvennom plane razvitiia narodnogo khoziaistva SSSR na 1973 god," *Pravda*, December 19, 1972, p. 3.

9. Dyker, *The Process of Investment*, p. 31.

10. M. Pessel, "Kredit kak faktor intensifikatsii kapital'nogo stroitel'stva," *Planovoe khoziaistvo*, no. 1 (1977): 51.

11. *Ibid.*

12. S. Bulgakov, "Metodologicheskaia osnova i problemy sozdaniia edinoi sistemy planirovaniia kapital'nogo stroitel'stva," *Ekonomika stroitel'stva*, no. 10 (1984): 12.

13. Dyker, *The Process of Investment*, pp. 37–8, 61–2.

14. V. Shavlyuk, "Pochemu dorozhaet stroika," *Pravda*, June 27, 2979, p. 2.

15. M. Cave and P. Hare, *Alternative Approaches to Economic Planning* (London: Macmillan, 1981), p. 152.

16. B. Z. Rumer, *Investment and Reindustrialization in the Soviet Economy* (Boulder and London: Westview Press, 1984), chapter 2.

17. V. Fil'ev, "Shchekinskii metod i perspektivy ego dal'neishego razvitiia," *Voprosy ekonomiki*, no. 2 (1983): 58–68.

18. See Dyker, *The Process of Investment*, pp. 45–6.

19. M. Z. Shakirov, "Povyshenie effektivnosti kapital'nogo stroitel'stva—zadacha veekh ego uchastnikov," *Ekonomika stroitel'stva*, no. 5 (1985): 14.

20. S. Bulgakov, "Nachinaetsia s plana," *Pravda*, September 7, 1987, p. 2.

21. R. B. Tian et al., "Sovershenstvovanie sistemy priniatiia reshenii pri razrabotke godovykh planov kapital'nogo stroitel'stva," *Ekonomika stroitel'stva*, no. 6 (1986): 33.

22. "V Tsentral'nom Komitate KPSS i Sovete Ministrov SSSR," *Ekonomicheskaia gazeta*, no. 23 (1984): 6–7.

23. N. Fedorenko, "Ekonomiko-matematicheskie modeli i metody,"

Ekonomicheskaia gazeta, no. 1 (1985): 14.

24. Tian, *op. cit.*, p. 33.

25. A. Deminov, "Novye smetnye normy i tseny," *Ekonomicheskaia gazeta*, no. 15 (1984): 8.

26. Iu. Batalin, "Perestroika nabiraet temp," *Ekonomicheskaia gazeta*, no. 1 (1987): 5.

27. "V Tsentral'nom Komitete KPSS i Sovete Ministrov SSSR," *Ekonomicheskaia gazeta*, no. 40 (1986): 9.

28. Batalin, *op. cit.*, p. 6.

29. *Ibid.*, p. 5.

30. I. Perepechin and L. Apraksina, "Kakov proekt—takov ob"ekt," *Ekonomicheskaia gazeta*, no. 6 (1980): 7.

31. A. G. Karnysh, "Effektivnyi put' sokrashcheniia investitsionnogo tsikla," *Ekonomika stroitel'stva*, no. 2 (1987): 13.

32. "O shirokom rasprostranenii novykh metodov khoziaistvovaniia i usilenii ikh vozdeistviia na uskorenie nauchno-tekhnicheskogo progressa," *Ekonomicheskaia gazeta*, no. 32 (1985), special supplement.

33. See D. A. Dyker, *The Future of the Soviet Economic Planning System* (London: Croom Helm, and New York, M. E. Sharpe, Inc., 1985), pp. 59–63.

34. B. Ural'tsev, "Otvetstvennost' vo vsekh zven'iakh," *Ekonomicheskaia gazeta*, no. 35 (1984): 8.

35. B. Tsagaraev, "Eksperiment i vstrechnyi," *Ekonomicheskaia gazeta*, no. 28 (1984): 8.

36. I. Iashkin, "Shagi v zavtra," *Pravda*, August 20, 1985, p. 2.

37. V. Moskalenko, "Samofinansirovanie kak metod ratsional'nogo khoziaistvovaniia," *Voprosy ekonomiki*, no. 1 (1986): 25.

38. P. Bunich, "Samofinansirovanie osnovnogo khoziaistvennogo zvena," *Voprosy ekonomiki*, no. 10 (1986): 19.

39. A. Rumiantsev and Iu. Goland, "Direktivnoe planirovanie i samostoiatel'nost' predpriiatii," *Ekonomicheskaia gazeta*, no. 4 (1987): 14–15.

40. See D. A. Dyker, "Planned and Unplanned Investment Patterns in the 1980s," in *The CMEA Five-Year Plans (1981–85) in a New Perspective* (Brussels: NATO Economics and Information Directorates, 1982).

41. See Hutchings, *op. cit.*, chapter 7.

42. See P. Hare, "Investment in Hungary: The Planners' Nightmare," paper presented at the NASEES annual conference, March 24–26, 1979, held at Fitzwilliam College, Cambridge.

43. See D. A. Dyker, "The Crisis in Yugoslav Self-Management," *Contemporary Review*, no. 242 (January 1983).

44. Dyker, *The Process of Investment*, pp. 63–4.

45. See, for example, G. Kulagin, "Trudno byt' universalom," *Pravda*, December 8, 1982, p. 2.

46. See M. E. Urban and J. McClure, "The Folklore of State Socialism: Semiotics and the Study of the Soviet State," *Soviet Studies*, vol. 35, no. 4 (October 1983).

PETER TOUMANOFF

Economic Reform and Industrial Performance in the Soviet Union 1950-1984

I. Introduction

This essay examines the evidence of the effects that reform efforts in the Soviet Union have had on industrial performance. Included in the reforms under investigation are the *sovnarkhozy* associated with Khrushchev, the reforms of plan indicators and supply relations associated with Kosygin, the re-emphasis on union ministries under Brezhnev and Kosygin, the integration of enterprises into production and scientific-production associations, and the formation of labor brigades in industry. Also considered is the possibility of a boss effect''—i.e., that regime changes by themselves affect industrial performance.

In each case, rationales for the reform and hypotheses about its effects are briefly surveyed. How far each reform was implemented is reported, and evidence of its effects is examined. The statistical evidence largely confirms the impression expressed in Western writings that reform attempts have been ineffective and, in some cases, counterproductive. Regime changes also appear not to have had an effect on industrial performance since 1950.

Industrial performance is measured as labor productivity in industry and as the rate of change of labor productivity. The effects of each reform and of regime changes are assessed via regression estimates that include as independent variables measures of reform implementation and of succession episodes.

The author teaches at Marquette University.

II. Economic Reform of Soviet Industry

Economic reform of Soviet industry has been motivated by steadily declining growth rates, chronic shortages in supply of intermediate products and consumer goods, persistent shortcomings in the quality of industrial products, and the apparent inability to generate and assimilate innovation in production processes. A likely explanation for these problems is that the Stalinist planning model cannot generate the information and incentives necessary to coordinate resource allocation effectively in a developed industrial sector. The range of possible remedies for the problems stretches from exhorting industrial personnel to improve their efforts within the existing framework of planning institutions to abandoning central planning altogether in favor of market mechanisms of allocating resources. Actual reform efforts have favored relatively minor tinkering with existing institutions while Western observers have suggested that anything short of major institutional reform is unlikely to be effective.[1]

There is considerable indirect evidence that reform efforts since Stalin's death have been unsuccessful. The decline in growth rates has continued unchecked, hitting bottom in 1982. Anecdotes of perverse managerial behavior, low worker morale, and shoddy products continue unabated. Attempts to assess Soviet progress in promoting technological change suggest that there has been none.[2] Perhaps the strongest indirect evidence that reforms have not been effective is the continued cycles of introduction–implementation–abandonment that have characterized reform since Stalin's death. We may know that reform has finally succeeded when Soviet leadership "steps off the treadmill" (as the cycle has been described by Gertrude Schroeder [1972 and 1983]).

Dyker (1985), Feiwel (1972), Ryavec (1975), and Schroeder (1972 and 1983) have discussed at length various reasons for the apparent failure of reform efforts. The consensus is that decentralization of the economic mechanism is necessary for reforms to be successful, and that reforms have not, in practice, decentralized. Decentralization is resisted for ideological, political, and bureaucratic reasons. Greater reliance on market signals implies a failure of socialism, reduces the political leverage that the Communist Party enjoys over the Soviet population, and threatens a powerful and entrenched economic bureaucracy. The result is a series of inappropriate and poorly integrated reforms, each one doomed to failure and abandoned when economic reality forces yet another reform attempt.

Khrushchev's Sovnarkhoz Experiment

The *sovnarkhoz* was a regional economic ministry, responsible for formulating and implementing economic plans for a region. Before 1957, when the regional ministries were instituted, the ministries were organized on a functional basis, and were criticized for failing to coordinate economic activity across industries within a geographic region. The *sovnarkhozy* relocated economic decision-making out of Moscow to the provinces. This move decentralized economic power at the ministerial level but not at the enterprise level. The change in location strengthened Khrushchev's political power but was not judged to be an economic success possibly because the political subdivisions to which the *sovnarkhozy* were attached were too small for rational economic allocation of resources.[3] Even the political advantage was short-lived. Resentment by bureaucrats sent out of Moscow contributed to the forces that ousted Khrushchev in October 1964.[4] The *sovnarkhoz* experiment was abandoned when Brezhnev and Kosygin came to power.

Implementation of the *sovnarkhoz* reform is measured by the percentage of industrial production in the Russian Soviet Federated Socialist Republic (RSFSR) that was carried out by enterprises under the direction of the regional ministries. The data are are reported and illustrated in Figure 1. To obtain a consistent series, the percentage reported for the RSFSR was used as a proxy for the entire nation. These data were obtained for the years 1957 to 1963 from the corresponding issues of *Narodnoe khoziaistvo SSSR*. The 1959 issue reports figures for both the USSR and the RSFSR. In 1958 and 1959 the percentage for the RSFSR is consistently five points higher than the percentage for the USSR. The use of the RSFSR data as a proxy for USSR data assumes that the bias is consistent throughout the period.

The Kosygin Reforms

A year after the succession of Khrushchev by Brezhnev and Kosygin a comprehensive set of changes known as the ''Kosygin reforms'' was announced. Their purpose was to improve managerial incentives to promote more efficient use of resources as well as innovation and reliability at the enterprise level. The announced components of the reform and the measures that were actually implemented have been extensively discussed elsewhere.[5] Important points that are made are

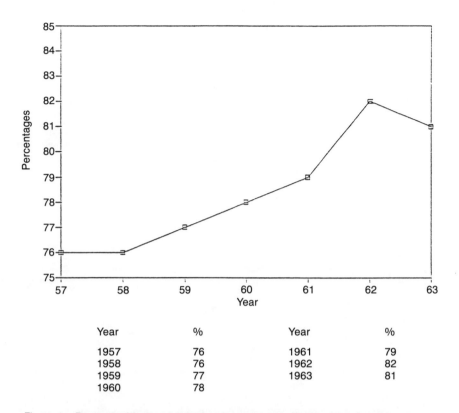

Year	%	Year	%
1957	76	1961	79
1958	76	1962	82
1959	77	1963	81
1960	78		

Figure 1   **Percent of Industrial Output Produced by Enterprises Subordinate to *Sovnarkhozy*.**

Source: *Narodnoe khoziaistvo*, 1957 through 1963.

these: (a) The reforms were a frequently contradictory mixture of centralizing and decentralizing features. In practice, industrial managers were subject to closer scrutiny of more plan targets, but at the same time were expected to demonstrate more initiative on investment decisions, innovations, supply links, and cost-cutting measures. (b) As the reform was carried out, the decentralizing features were sacrificed for the centralizing. The result was that by the early 1970s the organization of Soviet industry resembled fairly closely its pre-*sovnarkhoz* predecessor.[6] As was the case with the *sovnarkhozy*, economic goals were subordinate to political and bureaucratic reality.

According to the data published in *Narodnoe khoziaistvo*, by 1971 all of Soviet industry had transferred to the new system of controls. Figure 2 illustrates the implementation of the reform over time. Recognize that transferring all enterprises to the new system of controls does

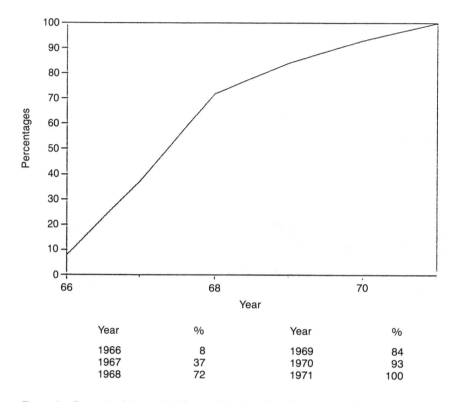

Year	%	Year	%
1966	8	1969	84
1967	37	1970	93
1968	72	1971	100

Figure 2   **Percent of Industrial Output Produced by Enterprises Subject to the Kosygin Reforms**

Source: *Narodnoe khoziaistvo*, 1966 through 1971.

not mean that the reform has been fully implemented. The controls themselves evolved over time and, as mentioned above, the features allowing for more managerial autonomy were largely discarded.

Union Ministries

At the same time that the Kosygin reforms were announced, union ministries were formed to replace the *sovnarkhozy*. Union ministries bring all enterprises in a particular branch of industry under the supervision of a single ministry responsible for the entire USSR. Production under the union ministry can be viewed as being more centrally directed than production under the republic ministries.[7] The purpose of the union ministry was to eliminate bureaucratic layers and so to streamline the operation of the enterprise. At the same time, the union minis-

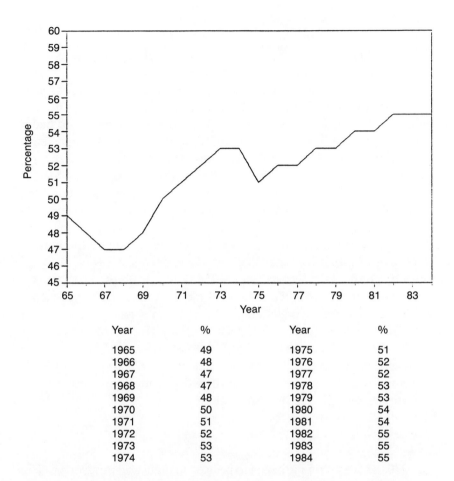

Year	%	Year	%
1965	49	1975	51
1966	48	1976	52
1967	47	1977	52
1968	47	1978	53
1969	48	1979	53
1970	50	1980	54
1971	51	1981	54
1972	52	1982	55
1973	53	1983	55
1974	53	1984	55

Figure 3 **Percent of Industrial Output Produced by Enterprises Subordinate to Union Ministries**

Source: *Narodnoe khoziaistvo*, 1965 through 1984.

tries were to permit enterprises enough autonomy to carry out the innovation and productivity goals of the Kosygin reforms.

As is evident from Figure 3, the transfer of enterprises to union ministries took place in 1965, and the percentage of output carried out under their aegis has increased relatively little since then. Perhaps the most interesting aspect of this transfer is that, despite intentions to the contrary, the union ministries were in most respects identical in power to the pre-*sovnarkhoz* industrial ministries. Decentralizing aspects of the new ministries were not implemented in practice.[8]

The Production Associations

The "production association," introduced in industry in 1970, is a new element in the Soviet economic hierarchy. The associations are horizontally and vertically integrated conglomerates of enterprises. This integration of enterprises represents increased centralization of economic power. At the same time the production associations are under *khozraschet* (that is, they are economically accountable) and represent a devolution of power from the ministries. Joseph Berliner (1976: 144) reports that the ministries resisted relinquishing power to the associations, thus diluting the decentralizing aspects of the reform. John Moore (1981: 204–5) argues that the objective of the production association was to economize on managerial costs, presumably by taking advantage of economies of scale in management. He suggests that their extensive adoption indicates that they have been successful. Another objective of the associations (especially the scientific-production association) was to improve the process of incorporating scientific discoveries into industrial production processes by integrating research and development facilities with production enterprises.

The data show that the adoption of the association by Soviet industry increased rapidly at first but has stagnated since 1978 at about half of all industrial production. Figure 4 illustrates the pattern of integration of enterprises into production associations.

Labor Brigades

In 1980 the labor brigade began to be used in industrial production. The labor brigade is a relatively small group of workers who work as a somewhat independent subcontracting production unit. In 1984, for example, each brigade averaged 12.1 workers.[9] The degree of independence varies among the type of brigade. The most independent form of brigade works under conditions of *khozraschet*. This form is the most effectively decentralized, and is expected to improve both quality of work and productivity of labor.[10] The other forms of brigade are not economically accountable, and workers are paid by a variety of means, including a piece-rate calculated according to a coefficient of work participation (*koeffitsient trudovogo uchastia*, KTU), and payment according to performance of some standard task. To the extent that these other forms of brigade are not operating under conditions of *khozraschet*, they represent less decentralized forms than the *khozraschet* bri-

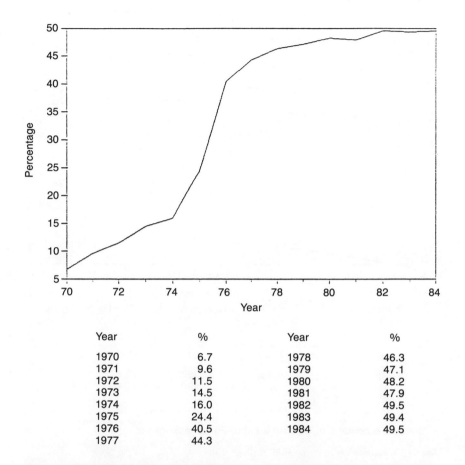

Year	%	Year	%
1970	6.7	1978	46.3
1971	9.6	1979	47.1
1972	11.5	1980	48.2
1973	14.5	1981	47.9
1974	16.0	1982	49.5
1975	24.4	1983	49.4
1976	40.5	1984	49.5
1977	44.3		

Figure 4   **Proportion of Industrial Output Produced by Production and Scientific-Production Associations**

Source: *Narodnoe khoziaistvo*, 1977 through 1984.

gade. Data are available on the percentage of the industrial labor force in both *khozraschet* brigades and the other kinds. These data are presented in Figure 5. They indicate that the brigade form in general is being rapidly adopted, and that the *khozraschet* form is the most rapidly growing.

Industrial Performance

Direct evidence of the effects of reform efforts on industrial performance can be provided by regression estimates of productivity and

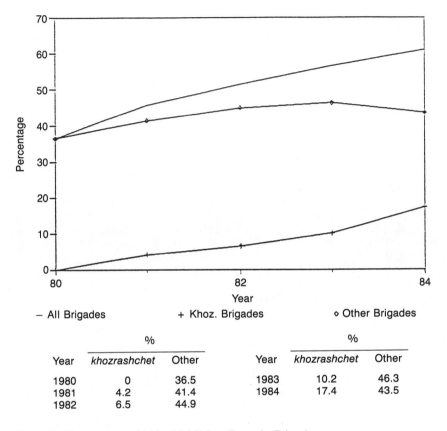

	%				%	
Year	*khozrashchet*	Other		Year	*khozrashchet*	Other
1980	0	36.5		1983	10.2	46.3
1981	4.2	41.4		1984	17.4	43.5
1982	6.5	44.9				

Figure 5   **Percentage of Industrial Labor Force in Brigades**

Source: Narodnoe khoziaistvo, 1980 through 1984.

growth equations if the measures of the implementation of reforms are included as explanatory variables. Regime changes must also be accounted for, because they may affect industrial performance, even apart from the reforms that frequently accompany them. New attitudes, new personnel, a heightened sense of insecurity, and discipline campaigns probably serve as a spur to management and industrial personnel. Alternatively, the disruption created by political change might reduce industrial productivity.

Existing production-function literature provides some guidance about appropriate design of the regression equations. Cameron (1981), Whitesell (1985), and Toumanoff (1985) have all found evidence that Soviet industrial production functions changed markedly sometime in the middle 1960s. Following Weitzman (1979), Desai (1985), and

Whitesell (1985), I specify the production function to be a Cobb-Douglas exhibiting constant returns to scale. The assumption of constant returns to scale allows output and factors of production to be expressed as ratios per unit of production worker. I include a quadratic trend variable to capture technological change, the variables discussed above to measure economic reform, and dummy variables to capture the effects of regime changes. The complete sample, 1950–1984, is split into the sub-periods 1950–1964 and 1965–1984 in order to take into account the structural changes in industrial production found by Cameron and Toumanoff. The earlier sub-period can measure the effects of the *sovnarkhoz* reform and the effects of Stalin's death, and the later sub-period can measure the effects of the Kosygin reforms, the union ministries, the production associations, the labor brigades, Khrushchev's ouster, and Brezhnev's death. Productivity growth is similarly modeled except that productivity and factor ratios are measured as percentage rates of change and the trend variable need not be quadratic. The complete specifications and a discussion of the data and methodology are reported in appendix A.

Hypotheses about the effects of reforms and regime changes on productivity and growth can be tested in two ways. First is simply to look at the coefficients estimated for the reform and regime-change variables. These are reported in tables B–1 through B–4 in appendix B. Insignificant coefficients confirm the hypothesis that reforms or regime changes had little effect on productivity or growth. Significantly positive coefficients indicate the possibility of a beneficial effect, while significantly negative coefficients indicate the possibility of a harmful effect. From Tables B–1 and B–2 it can be seen that both the *sovnarkhoz* and the regime change from Stalin to Khrushchev had insignificant effects on productivity and growth.[11] From Table B–3 it can be seen that the Kosygin reforms, the production associations, and the regime changes from Khrushchev to Brezhnev and from Brezhnev to Andropov had insignificant effects on productivity. Union ministries and other (non-*khozraschet*) forms of brigades are shown to have significantly negative effects on productivity, while the *khozraschet* form is shown to have a significantly positive effect in one specification (specification 2a). From Table B–4 it can be seen that all reform variables have insignificant effects on growth. While specification (3) lists a significantly negative coefficient for the change in regime to Brezhnev and a significantly positive coefficient for the change in regime to Andropov, this specification does not take into account the effects of the reforms.

The second method for testing hypotheses about the effects of reforms and regime changes is through the F-test comparisons also reported in Tables B–1 through B–4. Regression equations (2), (3), and (4) represent restricted versions of equation (1). Equation (2) restricts the value of the coefficients on regime-change variables to zero while accounting for reform; equation (3) restricts the value of the coefficients on reform variables to zero while accounting for regime changes; and equation (4) restricts the value of both reform and regime-change variables to zero. F-tests judge the significance of the restrictions. An insignificant F statistic validates the restriction.

Results of the F-test comparisons of the regression equations suggest the following. Neither the *sovnarkhoz* reform nor the change in regime from Stalin to Khrushchev significantly influenced industrial performance during the period 1950 to 1964. During the period 1965 to 1984 economic reforms did influence labor productivity. The union ministries and the non-*khozraschet* brigades reduced productivity while the *khozraschet* brigades increased productivity. Neither reforms nor regime changes influenced growth of productivity from 1950 to 1964.

Conclusion

The evidence presented in this paper confirms the analysis expressed by many that profound institutional reform of the Soviet economy is necessary to revitalize the stagnant industrial sector. Attempts at reform in the post-Stalin era have been insufficient, especially insofar as they have failed to decentralize economic decision- making. Of the reforms attempted, the union ministry and the non-*khozraschet* form of labor brigade appeared to decrease productivity. Only the most decentralized organizational form, the *khozraschet* form of labor brigade, appeared to have a beneficial effect on productivity. Other reforms appeared to have no effect at all. While the evidence is not absolutely conclusive, the case looks strong when the evidence of these regression estimates is combined with the indirect evidence of continued declines in industrial growth rates and continued calls for reform by the Soviets themselves.

Soviet leadership is surely aware of the record of industrial performance and of their attempts to reform it. It is another question altogether whether or not they have the will or the means necessary to carry out more profound reform. One can only be pessimistic about well-publicized but superficial efforts such as discipline campaigns and continued tinkering with the existing planning mechanism. My feeling is that a successfully decentralizing reform will take a generation to carry out and will not be particularly well-publicized. The bureaucracy and the party must have a stake in any successful reform, and the present generation of bureaucrats and party members have shown no such inclinations.

Appendix A: Regression Design and Data

Regression Design

I estimated four different regression equations for each period and for both labor productivity and growth of labor productivity. Each is a Cobb-Douglas production function exhibiting constant returns to scale and a quadratic trend variable. They differ in the reform and regime-change variables they include. For the period 1950–1964 the four equations are:

(1) $$Q/L = a_0 + a_1 K/L + a_2 TREND + a_3 TREND^2 + a_4 SOVNARKHOZ + a_5 KHRUSHCHEV + e$$

(2) $$b_0 + b_1 K/L + b_2 TREND + b_3 TREND^2 + b_4 SOVNARKHOZ + e$$

(3) $$Q/L = c_0 + c_1 K/L + c_2 TREND + c_3 TREND^2 + c_4 KHRUSHCHEV + e$$

(4) $$Q/L = d_0 + d_1 K/L + d_2 TREND + d_3 TREND^2 + e$$

where Q/L equals labor productivity, K equals capital stock, and L equals production workers. Output and factors of production are all expressed as ratios per unit of production worker in order to impose constant returns to scale on the production function. All ratios are expressed as logarithms. The trend variable, TREND, is measured as the year. SOVNARKHOZ is the proportion (expressed as a decimal) of total output produced under the direction of *sovnarkhozy* in the RSFSR, as reported in Figure 1. The dummy variable KHRUSHCHEV takes the value one for the years 1954 and 1955 and zero for all other observations. I experimented with all the possible definitions of this variable from the years 1954 to 1958, and the chosen one provided the lowest residual sum of squares. The growth equations are identical, with the exception that Q/L and K/L are measured as percentage rates of change and $TREND^2$ is unnecessary.

The four equations for the period from 1965 to 1984 are:

(1) $$Q/L = a_0 + a_1 K/L + a_2 TREND + a_3 TREND^2$$
$$+ a_4 KOSREFORM + a_5 UNION$$
$$+ a_6 ASSOCIATION + a_7 BRIGONE$$
$$+ a_8 BRIGTWO + a_9 BREZHNEV$$
$$+ a_{10} ANDROPOV + e,$$

(2) $$Q/L = b_0 + b_1 K/L + b_2 TREND + b_3 TREND^2$$
$$+ b_4 KOSREFORM + b_5 UNION$$
$$+ b_6 ASSOCIATION + b_7 BRIGONE$$
$$+ b_8 BRIGTWO + e$$

(3) $$Q/L = c_0 + c_1 K/L + c_2 TREND + c_3 TREND^2$$
$$+ c_4 BREZHNEV + c_5 ANDROPOV + e$$

(4) $$Q/L = d_0 + d_1 K/L + d_2 TREND + d_3 TREND^2 + e$$

where Q/L, K, L, and TREND are as above. KOSREFORM, UNION, ASSO-CIATION, BRIGONE, and BRIGTWO measure the implementation of the Kosygin reforms, union ministries, production associations, *khozraschet* brigades, and other brigades, respectively. All are as reported in their respective tables, in decimal form. BREZHNEV takes the value one in the years 1965 and 1966 and zero elsewhere, and ANDROPOV takes the value one in the years 1983 and 1984 and zero elsewhere. These capture the two years immediately following regime changes. The growth equations are identical with the same exceptions noted above for 1950–1964.

Data

The data were collected from the appropriate volumes of the Central Statistical Administration publication *Narodnoe khoziaistvo SSSR*. While I recognize the well-documented shortcomings of Soviet data, it is sufficient for the purposes of this investigation if the biases inherent in the output, capital, and labor data are not systematically related to the reform or regime-change variables this investigation focuses on. Where there are such biases, they may be expected to overstate the contributions of the reforms. Since this investigation found the reforms (with but one exception) ineffective or harmful, such a bias is unimportant for its conclusions.

Appendix B: Regression Results

In the following tables are the regression coefficients and summary statistics estimated for the equations described in Appendix A. Also included are the results of the F-test comparisons of the estimates. Several methodological notes are addressed below.

1. Each estimate was made under the assumption of variable returns to scale as well as the constant returns to scale estimates reported below. Restricting the production function to constant returns to scale was validated by F-tests in each case.

2. Data were unavailable for the proportion of industry under the direction of *sovnarkhozy* for the year 1964. Because it is known that they were not abolished until October of 1965, I extrapolated a value of 80 percent for that year. The signs and significance of the regression estimates were not sensitive to values for that year, ranging from 0 to 85 percent.

3. Two sets of estimates are reported for the productivity equations for the period 1965–1984. Estimates (1), (2), (3), and (4) are ordinary least-squares estimates. The Durbin-Watson statistics for those estimates lead one to suspect serial correlation of the error terms. Estimates (1a), (2a), (3a), and (4a) are maximum-likelihood estimates of the same equations. My judgment is that the maximum-likelihood estimators are the more efficient.

Table B–1

Regression Coefficients and Summary Statistics
Labor Productivity: 1950–1964

Independent variable	Specification			
	(1)	(2)	(3)	(4)
CONSTANT	3.29*	3.30*	3.27*	3.28*
K/L	−.00079	.00043	−.0040	−.0029
TREND	.090*	.089*	.089*	.091*
TREND²	−.0016*	−.0016*	−.0017*	−.0016*
SOVNARKHOZ	.0099	.013		
KHRUSHCHEV	−.0029		−.0060	
R²	.999	.999	.999	.999
Durbin-Watson	1.79	1.76	1.70	1.38

F-Test Comparison of Specifications

Specifications	Null hypothesis	F-statistic	Outcome
1 and 4	Political succession and economic reform have no effect	$F(2,9) = .73$	Accepted
1 and 3	Economic reform has no effect, taking into account succession	$F(1,9) = .55$	Accepted
1 and 2	Political succession has no effect, taking into account reform	$F(1,9) = .15$	Accepted

*Significant at 5% level of confidence.

Table B–2

Regression Coefficients and Summary Statistics
Productivity Growth: 1951–1964

Independent variable	Specification			
	(1)	(2)	(3)	(4)
CONSTANT	.089*	.092*	.088*	.092*
K/L	.0086	.0059	.0092	.0060
TREND	−.0039*	−.0034*	−.0030*	−.0033*
SOVNARKHOZ	.00011	.000004		
KHRUSHCHEV	.013		.011	
R²	.811	.748	.798	.748
Durbin-Watson	1.83	1.83	1.71	1.38

F-Test Comparison of Specifications

Specifications	Null hypothesis	F-statistic	Outcome
1 and 4	Political succession and economic reform have no effect	$F(2,9) = 1.48$	Accepted
1 and 3	Economic reform has no effect, taking into account succession	$F(1,9) = .61$	Accepted
1 and 2	Political succession has no effect, taking into account reform	$F(1,9) = 2.96$	Accepted

*Significant at 5% level of confidence.

Table B-3

Regression Coefficients and Summary Statistics
Labor Productivity: 1965–1984

Independent variable				Specification				
	(1)	(1a)**	(2)	(2a)**	(3)	(3a)**	(4)	(4a)**
CONSTANT	9.28*	9.36*	8.93*	8.39*	8.63*	7.79*	7.56*	6.65*
K/L	1.03*	1.04*	.968*	.892*	.946*	.799*	.772*	.616*
TREND	.041	.040	.047	.059*	.042	.048*	.055*	.063*
TREND^2	-.0012*	-.0012*	-.0012*	-.0013*	-.0011*	-.0011*	-.0011*	-.0011*
KOSREFORM	-.012	-.014	-.0024	-.017				
UNION	-.426*	-.431*	-.520*	-.528*				
ASSOCIATION	.046	.043	.033	.018				
BRIGONE	.165	.139	.217	.246*				
BRIGTWO	-.037	-.040*	-.041	-.048*				
BREZHNEV	-.014	-.015			-.010	-.014		
ANDROPOV	.0091	.012			.014	.011		
R^2	.999	.999	.999	.999	.999	.999	.999	.999
Durbin-Watson	3.00	2.79	2.90	2.71	1.14	1.73	1.09	1.63

F-Test Comparison of Specifications

Specifications	Null hypothesis	F-statistic	Outcome
1 and 4	Political succession and economic reform have no effect	$F_{(7,9)} = 4.69^*$	Rejected
1 and 3	Economic reform has no effect, taking into account succession	$F_{(5,9)} = 5.30^*$	Rejected
1 and 2	Political succession has no effect, taking into account reform	$F_{(2,9)} = .995$	Accepted

*Significant at 5% level of confidence.
**Maximum–likelihood estimate.

Table B-4

Regression Coefficients and Summary Statistics
Productivity Growth: 1965-1984

Independent variable	Specification			
	(1)	(2)	(3)	(4)
CONSTANT	−.028	.0094	.088*	.059*
K/L	.182	.158	.425*	.522*
TREND	.0015	.0024	−.0027*	−.0018
KOSREFORM	−.014	.0017		
UNION	.122	−.016		
ASSOCIATION	−.092	−.107		
BRIGONE	−.053	.027		
BRIGTWO	−.026	−.029		
BREZHNEV	−.016		−.017*	
ANDROPOV	.013		.016*	
R²	.802	.776	.753	.618
Durbin-Watson	2.41	2.51	2.04	1.70

F-Test Comparison of Specifications

Specifications	Null hypothesis	F-statistic	Outcome
1 and 4	Political succession and economic reform have no effect	$F(7,10) = 1.33$	Accepted
1 and 3	Economic reform has no effect taking into account succession	$F(5,10) = .50$	Accepted
1 and 2	Political succession has no effect, taking into account reform	$F(2,10) = .68$	Accepted

*Significant at 5% level of confidence.

Notes

Support from the Bradley Institute for Democracy and Public Values is gratefully acknowledged by the author.

1. Among the Western observers calling for major institutional reform are Goldman (1983), Berliner (1976), Cocks (1983), Dyker (1981 and 1985), and Granick (1983).

2. See Weitzman (1970), Bergson (1979 and 1983), Berliner (1976), Desai (1985), and Toumanoff (1985) for evidence of declining rates of technical change. Desai and Martin (1983) find that the overall efficiency of resource allocation in Soviet industry has declined. Cameron (1981) finds, in contrast, an acceleration in the pace of technological change since 1967.

3. See Dyker (1985), p. 43.

4. See Bernard (1966), pp. 108–36 and Heller and Nekrich (1986), pp. 553–54.

5. See, for example, Feiwel (1972), Ryavec (1975), Dyker (1985), and Schroeder (1972).

6. An exception was the freedom of the enterprise to engage in decentralized investment. This feature of the Kosygin reforms was very popular with the enterprises and had to be limited because of its tendency to promote autarky. See Dyker (1985), pp. 61–62.

7. See Gorlin and Doane (1983), p. 419.

8. See Ryavec (1975), pp. 60–85.

9. See *Narodnoe khoziaistvo* (1984: 144) as an example.

10. See Dyker (1985: 114) on the "Zlobin" (*khozraschet*) brigade in construction.

11. Recognizing that the change from Stalin to Khrushchev took four years of political maneuvering, I experimented with a variety of definitions of the dummy variable associated with Khrushchev. Identifying 1954 and 1955 as the years associated with the regime change performed best.

References

Bergson, Abram (1979). "Notes on the Production Function in Soviet Postwar Industrial Growth," *Journal of Comparative Economics* 3 (June): 116–26.

———— (1983). "Technological Progress." In A. Bergson and H. Levine (eds.), *The Soviet Economy: Toward the Year 2000*. London: Allen and Unwin.

Berliner, Joseph (1976). *The Innovation Decision in Soviet Industry*. Cambridge: The MIT Press.

Bernard, Philippe J.; trans. by I. Nove (1966). *Planning in the Soviet Union*. Oxford: Pergamon Press.

Cameron, Norman E. (1981). "Economic Growth in the USSR, Hungary, and East and West Germany," *Journal of Comparative Economics* 5 (March): 24–42.

Cocks, Paul (1983). "Organizing for Technological Innovation in the 1980s." In Gregory Guroff and Fred Carstensen (eds.), *Entrepreneurship in Imperial Russia and the Soviet Union*. Princeton: Princeton University Press, pp. 306–46.

Desai, Padma (1985). "Total Factor Productivity in Postwar Soviet Industry and Its Branches," *Journal of Comparative Economics* 9, no. 1 (March): 1–23.

Desai, Padma, and Ricardo Martin (1983). "Efficiency Loss from Resource Misallocation in Soviet Industry," *Quarterly Journal of Economics* (August): 441–56.

Dyker, David A. (1981). "Decentralization and the Command Principle—Some Lessons from Soviet Experience," *Journal of Comparative Economics* 5 (June): 121–48.

———— (1985). *The Future of the Soviet Economic Planning System*. Armonk, N.Y.: M. E. Sharpe, Inc.

Feiwel, George R. (1972). *The Soviet Quest for Economic Efficiency: Issues, Controversies, and Reforms*. New York: Praeger Publishers.

Goldman, Marshall I. (1983). *USSR in Crisis: The Failure of an Economic System*. New York: W. W. Norton & Co.

Gorlin, Alice C., and David P. Doane (1983). "Plan Fulfillment and Growth in Soviet Ministries," *Journal of Comparative Economics* 7, no. 4 (December) 415–31.

Granick, David (1983). "Institutional Innovation and Economic Management: The Soviet Incentive System, 1921 to the Present." In Gregory Guroff and Fred Carstensen (eds.), *Entrepreneurship in Imperial Russia and the Soviet Union*. Princeton: Princeton University Press, pp. 223–37.

Heller, Mikhail, and Aleksandr Nekrich (1986). *Utopia in Power: The History of the Soviet Union from 1917 to the Present*. New York: Summit Books.

Moore, John H. (1981). "Agency Costs, Technological Change, and Soviet Central Planning," *Journal of Law and Economics* 24, no. 2 (October): 189–214.

Ryavec, Karl W. (1975). *Implementation of Soviet Economic Reforms: Political, Organizational, and Social Processes.* New York: Praeger Publishers.

Schroeder, Gertrude (1983). "Soviet Economic 'Reform' Decrees: More Steps on the Treadmill." In Joint Economic Committee, *Soviet Economy in the 1980s: Problems and Prospects, Part I.* Washington: U.S. Government Printing Office.

———— (1972). "The 'Reform' of the Supply System in Soviet Industry," *Soviet Studies* 24, no. 1 (July): 97–119.

Toumanoff, Peter (1985). "An Investigation of Soviet Industrial Reform," *Soviet Union/Union Sovietique* 12, p. 2: 152–60.

Tsentral'nyi Statisticheskoe Upravlenie. *Narodnoe khoziaistvo SSSR.* Moscow: Statistika, 1951—.

Weitzman, Martin L. (1979). "Technology Transfer to the USSR: An Econometric Analysis," *Journal of Comparative Economics* 3: 167–77.

Whitesell, Robert S. (1985). "The Influence of Central Planning on the Economic Slowdown in the Soviet Union and Eastern Europe: A Comparative Production Function Analysis," *Economica* 52: 235–44.

SUSAN J. LINZ

The Impact of Soviet Economic Reform
Evidence from the Soviet Interview Project

I. Introduction

Since the initial economic reform proposals in 1965, Soviet leaders have periodically announced a series of measures to improve both the efficiency of resource utilization and the quality of output.[1] In her description of the "treadmill" of Soviet economic reforms, Schroeder (1979, p. 313) draws "a road map through the labyrinthian maze that has been created by the reformed and reforming reforms of the organizational arrangements and incentive rules." Despite the continuous process of reforming the reforms over the past two decades, productivity growth and product quality remain low. Soviet leaders appear to share the view that they have yet to find the particular combination of reform measures capable of reversing the downward trend in productivity and improving product quality. Indeed, Gorbachev stepped onto the "treadmill" during his first year in office, calling for organizational and incentive structure changes (Hanson 1986, Hewett 1986, Hough 1986, Schroeder 1986).

Western economists generally regard the undramatic effect of the numerous changes as stemming from inconsistencies in, and limited introduction of, the reforms (Campbell 1968; Abouchar 1973; Schroeder 1972, 1973, 1979; Dyker 1981, 1983; Hanson 1983). Relying on official pronouncements, however, may not accurately portray the scope of Soviet reform efforts. In-depth interviews with recent Soviet emigrants who held managerial positions in planning, production, and supply organizations offer valuable insight into actual reform practices. Such insight is not forthcoming from official sources.

The author teaches at Michigan State University.

This paper summarizes results gathered from intensive interviews with 53 expert informants, individuals who formerly held responsible positions in the Soviet economic bureaucracy. Informants reported on their experience with the economic reforms of the 1960s and 1970s; some volunteered experiences with the *sovnarkhozy*, introduced by Khrushchev in 1957.[2]

In accordance with the general theme of hierarchical reform in the Soviet economic bureaucracy, this paper focuses on those responses dealing with organizational change. Informants were asked questions about how the reforms affected organizational arrangements within their enterprise, and about the Shchekino experiment, in particular. In an effort to delineate the impact of the reforms on the relationship between industrial enterprises, informants were asked how production associations (*proizvodstvennye ob"edineniia*) affected planning, production, or the availability of supplies, and whether the ministry encouraged their enterprise to establish "direct links" with other firms. Informants reported on the impact of the reforms on the planning process in general, and on the planning of supply and distribution of materials, in particular. Finally, informants were asked if (and how) the reforms affected enterprise-ministry relations or the functions of the ministry.

II. Value of Qualitative Data

Intensive interviews with expert informants are not widely used by economists. Qualitative, or anecdotal, evidence usually implies that the observations are not randomly collected and are not sufficiently numerous to identify a systematic pattern of behavior. Yet, because current research in economics focuses on information and uncertainty, the role of qualitative research is growing. Qualitative data are useful in providing information to reduce uncertainty in specifying relationships among economic agents, and in spelling out the nature of the uncertainty a particular agent faces. Further, qualitative data shed light on how agents acquire the knowledge that economists attribute to them. Such data offer a way of discovering how economic agents interpret or think about the world, enabling the researcher to formulate and test hypotheses about what part of the world agents pay attention to when making decisions.

Can one generalize the results obtained from qualitative research? When one wants to generalize from a sample to some larger population (how many individuals eat breakfast or smoke, for example), random sampling is the appropriate strategy. Random sampling increases the likelihood that the data collected are representative of the entire population of interest. Sample size is determined by the size of the population to which one wants to generalize, the expected amount of variation in the population, and the amount of error one is willing to accept. When one wants to learn something in particular (whether managers initiate innovation, for example), purposeful sampling is the best strategy (select only those individuals who hold managerial positions, or who are in direct and frequent contact with managers).

For the enterprise management study, conducted under the auspices of the Soviet Interview Project,[3] few individuals with the requisite work experience were available. Of the 37,000 Soviet emigrants who arrived in the United States between 1979 and 1982, only two dozen were identified as former enterprise directors; fewer than 150 held top-level management positions. Moreover, financial constraints restricted sample size. To deal with the problem of representativeness under conditions of small sample size, I elected to maximize the variation in respondents' work experience (across relevant occupations, economic branches, and geographic regions) in order to have more confidence in those patterns that might emerge as common among respondents. Selecting the sample to maximize the breadth in work environments also makes it possible to document unique work-related experiences. Table 1 identifies the sample by occupation: forty informants held managerial positions, some reporting on two work environments. Table 2 illustrates the distribution of work experience in different sectors of the Soviet economic bureaucracy. More detailed discussion of the sample selection process is provided elsewhere (Linz 1986).

Can one generalize results obtained from intensive interviews with former Soviet citizens who have emigrated to the United States? Despite efforts to select a sample representative of Soviet enterprise management and the assistance of interviewers trained by the National Opinion Research Center (NORC), two potential sources of bias remain. First, the process of leaving the USSR or living in the US ("emigrant bias") may affect responses. Second, the majority of respondents were Jewish ("ethnic bias"). The problem of bias in a sample of Soviet emigrants has been treated extensively elsewhere (Millar 1987). Here it suffices to say that emigrant bias was minimized in the enterprise management study by asking informants about their work experience and environment before their decision to emigrate.

Table 1

Enterprise Management Sample: Occupation*

Occupation	Number of respondents
Management	
Director	6
Assistant director	3
Head of planning or financial department	14
Assistant department head	5
Head of technical-manufacturing section, group, bureau, other	7
Leading personnel in supply or sales organization	5
Staff and Other	
Economic planners and economists	8
Accountants	2
Engineers	8
Agents, forwarders, controllers	2

*Eight respondents reported on two occupations.

Table 2

Enterprise Management Sample: Economic Branch[a]

Economic Branch	Number of respondents
Heavy industry[b]	16
Light industry[c]	13
Construction, transportation	10
Commerce, material-technical supply	7
Other[d]	15

a. Six informants reported on two branches; one reported on three.

b. Includes construction materials, machine building, chemical, heat insulating material, aircraft, synthetic fiber, energy.

c. Includes textiles, sewing, printing, distillery, pharmaceuticals, toys, glue, synthetic rubber goods.

d. Includes research institutes, government planning and financial organizations, agriculture.

Although ethnic bias is unavoidable given the nature of the "third emigration," it appears to be a selective bias that pertains to questions related to ethnicity and not to more general economic or political questions (Bahry 1985).

Because interview data are best suited for revealing patterns of responses, individual responses cannot be interpreted in isolation. Responses must be grouped together and taken as a whole in order to function as clues to the decision-making process in Soviet enterprises. Space constraints prohibit providing detailed responses by all informants to questions pertaining to hierarchical reform in the Soviet economic bureaucracy. An extensive presentation of the interview data underlying this paper is available from the Soviet Interview Project (Linz 1987).

Management's Perception of the "Treadmill"

Over half of the informants were asked about their experiences with the reforms of the 1960s and 1970s, and, in particular, about the "most significant reform" introduced while they were working. Of these individuals, fourteen worked in industrial enterprises (eight in heavy industry); ten worked in construction, transportation, or supply organizations; three worked in planning or other government organizations. On the whole, the informants formerly working in heavy industry (nearly all of whom were head of the planning department in their enterprise), construction and transportation were more informed or more willing to talk about the reforms.

We didn't really have a reform. We were preparing it, but it was never ratified. . . . Enterprises were often reorganized, one reform after another, and we had no time to follow them. Maybe that was the reason nothing changed.

It's only words that the enterprise can . . . be more independent.

Everything always begins well, looks great on paper, but then the system itself ruins everything.

In the country as a whole, the biggest reform was when we changed to regional economic administrations (*sovnarkhozy*). . . . It was an outrageous system.

They only poured water from one bottle to another. . . . In practice nothing changed. . . . One time they tried to give more rights to the enterprises . . . but they became afraid of private enterprise and stopped it.

Liberman . . . created a whole system in which the enterprise would have an incentive to make a profit. They introduced it almost everywhere, but then they changed it so much that it didn't even resemble itself.

The reforms did not increase productivity, nor did they increase production. The reasons are found in the very structure of the system. I also thought about this: why in the presence of good specialists and workers don't you get anything? I think the structure itself is guilty.

The reforms that were introduced were modified—dozens of new instructions from the ministry. Even if the reform had good goals, these instructions brought it to naught.

Interview data reveal a general consensus among managers regarding the failure of the reforms to increase productivity. Managers in this study reported at length on the difficulties they faced with the lack of labor discipline and labor turnover, and shortages of materials and labor, all of which contribute to the low productivity of workers. Similar results were obtained by the General Survey of the Soviet Interview Project.[4] Of the 766 respondents asked whether labor productivity was declining in the USSR (more than three-quarters of whom said yes), 191 held positions comparable to those who participated in the enterprise management project. That is, they held "managerial" positions in manufacturing, transportation, construction, trade, and material-technical supply. As shown in Table 3, three out of four top-level managers ("leaders") viewed productivity declining; four out of five of the engineer-technical staff, people in direct contact with workers, shared this view.[5]

When asked "what kind of reform would have worked best to improve the performance of your enterprise?" the majority response offered by participants in the enterprise management project, interviewed before Gorbachev's appointment as General Secretary, focused on giving more independence to enterprises.

A factory needs independence. Centralized planning is good, but . . . practically speaking, all of the employees had their hands tied. They couldn't do anything outside the plan.

Table 3

Was Labor Productivity Declining in the USSR?
(Soviet Interview Project: General Survey)

Respondents	Yes (True)	No (Not True)	Row total
Leaders[a]	22	7	29
Other managers[b]	15	6	21
High engineer-technical (ITR)[c]	37	10	47
Low ITR; other professional[d]	66	28	94
Column Total	140	51	191

a. The "leaders" in the General Survey who responded to this question were distributed across the following sectors: 15 in manufacturing (8 in heavy industry, 3 in light industry, 4 in other industry); 4 in transportation; 9 in construction; 1 in trade.

b. "Other managers" worked in manufacturing (3), transportation and construction (4), trade (12), and material-technical supply (2).

c. "High" engineer-technical personnel had work experience in machine building (21), light and other industry (4), transportation and material-technical supply (4), and construction (18).

d. "Low" engineer-technical personnel and other professionals worked in manufacturing (21 in heavy industry, 14 in light industry, 4 in other industry), transportation (3), construction (14), trade (28), and material-technical supply (3).

The general consensus among these informants, however, was that "such reforms are impossible in the Soviet Union because they would allow too much freedom."

A general question about the impact of the reforms in the 1960s and 1970s on organizational methods in the production or work of enterprises yielded so little response that frequently it was omitted during the interview, or replaced by a more specific question about the Shchekino experiment. All those asked were familiar with the Shchekino experiment, but did not take it seriously.

From time to time there suddenly arises some noise in the papers that a brigade of communist labor has taken upon itself new obligations. . . . They exhibit it as an example, and they take care of supplying it with necessary equipment and supplies . . . They say it is possible to work like this, but to supply everybody with the necessary materials is impossible.

I worked on this. Our enterprise was free to choose the number of people and to pay more salary by hiring fewer people. For the same job, people made more money. It was about ten years ago. It was difficult to implement because nobody wanted to risk not fulfilling the plan. . . . It is hard work . . . We didn't want to participate. Our workers said: "If you punish us for not participating in the experiment, we will apply for work elsewhere, where it is safer for us.'' Consequently, we had to post a special notice that at five work stations there would be 12 workers instead of 10, and at another station there would be 5 workers instead of 12 because at that station we could do it. . . .

This system was very nice. There was more freedom. . . . But as time went on, the banks said: ''This is not good. You paid one worker 250 rubles, and another worker 100 rubles for the same work.'' . . . If all people receive more money, they need more clothes, more education, more and more of everything—television, cars. And the government cannot give these things.

The Shchekino system was designed to give directors more freedom, more power to decide about workers and salaries. The planners . . . realized that it would cause unemployment. . . . The Shchekino method died before it was born.

Several features stand out in the interview evidence regarding management's perception of the ''treadmill'' of Soviet economic reforms. First, the relative youth of light industry managers was such that they were not familiar with enough different reforms to get a sense of the ''treadmill.'' Even though heavy industry managers appeared to be more knowledgeable, general questions about the 1965 reforms and those in the 1970s elicited little response. Similar results would no doubt obtain if U.S. managers were asked, for example, about their experience with the monetary policy reform in 1979. Managers in both systems are better able to report how their decisions or actions changed as a consequence of changes in their work environment. Managers in this sample, with the exception of those who had experience with *sovnarkhozy*, reported little change in their work environment beyond that associated with technological advance.

Second, Soviet managers cite greater enterprise autonomy and the corresponding increase in competition as *potentially* the most significant reform. This may stem from their experiences in the United States or from their reaction to the onslaught of articles on private enterprise in the Soviet press. It is not the case, however, that they reject the centralized system. In some cases, informants viewed greater centralization as the solution to supply problems. Moreover, most informants had what they considered to be relatively well-paying jobs, and a reasonable standard of living.[6] Third, managers in this sample expressed concern at what they perceived as a lack of interest in quality by both planners and workers. They attributed poor performance (and low productivity) to an attitude toward work they characterized as stemming from a lack of self-interest or responsibility on the part of the workers. Such concerns are not uncommon among production or project managers in Western industrialized societies.

Fourth, managers expressed doubt that anything less than a major reform of the Soviet system would improve enterprise operation or performance. Such a reform in their view, however, is unlikely because too many individuals at all levels of the economic bureaucracy are successfully ''working'' the system.

III. Reforms Alter Relationships between Enterprises

Organizational restructuring of the Soviet economic bureaucracy in the 1970s had an impact on the relationships between enterprises in two important ways. First, enterprises and research organizations were merged into large corporate units called associations (ob"edineniia).[7] Second, enterprises were encouraged to establish ''direct links'' with other organizations. Giving managers the right to establish contracts directly with other firms would facilitate production and distribution processes by reducing the need to rely on ministry mediation.

Thirty-eight informants queried about their experience with production associations (19 in heavy industry, construction and transportation; 10 in light industry; 9 in planning, supply, and research organizations) reported on both the positive and negative aspects. The diversity of experience among the informants is highlighted in the following excerpts:

. . . not a bad idea . . . ''allowed for'' specialization in production.

Experienced people worked in the ob"edineniia . . . who were able to manage it effectively. But it was also the case that ob"edineniia were managed by party organizations, by people inexperienced in production.

. . . curtails the size of the government apparatus . . . permits local redistribution of resources to help needy enterprises.

. . . symbolic organizations . . . enterprises were responsible for production . . . most important is the production unit, the enterprise.

Very little changed ''as a result of the associations.'' However, it is easier now for small enterprises . . . if they need materials, we give it to them, because for us it is only a small amount. Since we do not have nearly enough to fulfill our plan anyway, this amount is not important. But it helps them to fulfill their plan.

"The association" has little authority. The ministry really was in charge. . . . It was too much freedom. . . . We got numbers we could juggle between factories. How we distributed the figures really depended upon our mood: which factory we liked, which we didn't.

. . . problems were solved much faster in the *ob"edineniia* . . . even planning became more stable. . . . It is difficult to prove that the enterprise is right . . . They "superior organizations" consider themselves right. They were sure we had hidden reserves . . . that we worked badly, that we had to be more creative, that our technologists worked badly.

The idea behind this was to save money on administrative salaries, and to centralize. . . . "a plan is" divided up among different factories rather than doing parallel jobs in each factory. The supply system can also be centralized. . . . It made it more comfortable for overall management, but more difficult for the enterprise director.

We united enterprises which were far away from each other—eight to ten hours away. How can you speak of control under such conditions? I practically could not control them and restricted myself to sending plans to them and demanding the achievement of these plans. . . . I think the *ob"edineniia* can offer a positive influence if "they" make one single supply center, really make things centralized.

It hindered the flexibility of the enterprise.

It became easier to plan merchandise assortment. . . . distribution of merchandise became more fair . . . but it worsened the situation for stores who previously were affiliated with a particular firm—they lost their advantages.

I can't say that they were a big help. They just gathered "plan" indicators, and sometimes they were even a hindrance.

They were mostly for show, with little real content.

There was more power in fewer hands, but subordinate organizations lost their responsibility. . . . This reform was supposed to reduce the ratio between office employees and workers . . . but this did not happen.

I think there was an easier and better relationship between people when it was a small company, before the *ob"edineniia*. . . . All the changes "when *ob"e-dineniia* were introduced" were in management control. . . . In practice, it didn't change much.

Reducing the number of administrative personnel was a positive aspect, only "large eats small." If there is one large factory, the smaller factories "in the *ob"edineniia*" will not get the same materials—it won't even have a bank account in order to help make decisions. . . . If the factory is not located at the center, its plans are modified depending upon what is happening in the main enterprise.

It is not the case that positive (or negative) sentiments can be linked with a particular sector or industry; nor are they directly linked to individuals who worked in *ob"edineniia* as opposed to those who did not. On a general level, the variation in the answers can be grouped into two categories—those who thought the production associations were a good idea that did not work; and those who thought they were a bad idea.

From management's perspective, the production associations were a failure. Despite what they believed to be the goals of the reorganization of the economic bureaucracy, in their view the overall size of bureaucracy grew. Yet power remained in the hands of the ministry. The most common complaint in light industry was that the *ob"edineniia* reduced the ability of enterprises to respond to consumer demand. Furthermore, the introduction of *ob"edineniia* did not result in more control over production or distribution. One informant, in a rather exaggerated statement, reports that styles (fashions) changed before the planning paperwork made it through the bureaucratic hierarchy. Informants working in *ob"edineniia* called for more control, especially over the supply of materials to enterprises. Two informants working in *ob"edineniia* specified an inverse relationship between the location of enterprises subordinate to their organization and their ability to control. In their view, control meant physically being there, and with enterprises so far apart, that was not possible. Managers, especially those working in the *ob"edineniia,* reported more shuffling of plan targets among enterprises based upon somewhat arbitrary decision rules.

The relationship between firms in the Soviet economic bureaucracy was also affected by the introduction of "direct links." The reliance on "direct links" between enterprises was designed to decentralize the supply system. Ministry and other planning officials were initially to identify supply-client relationships between enterprises, giving enterprises the responsibility to maintain such relationships over time. Soviet sources report a significant increase in the number of firms engaged in "direct links,"[8] but it is not clear in the literature whether such linkages increased enterprise autonomy, or improved the timing or quantity of supplies to the enterprise. It appears that contracts between enterprises have no allowance for price setting, thus suppliers need not be responsive to clients' needs. But the literature is unclear as to what happens if a delivery contract is violated.

Thirty informants (3 directors, 3 assistant directors, 9 department heads, 5 assistant department heads, 10 staff and other) were asked whether the ministry encouraged their enterprise to contact other firms directly, to establish "direct links." Several reported on their experience with "direct links" between enterprises:

. . . special agreements were made between enterprises. In these agreements, the deadlines for deliveries were specified, as well as a level of responsibility that each enterprise carries for delays of deliveries or payments. This was designed to help the enterprises, but oftentimes these enterprises conflicted with each other, since each one was trying to blame the other for failing to fulfill the agreement. In the end, everyone turned to the ministry, or the ministry turned to another "cooperative enterprise," or some sanctions were imposed in order to speed up deliveries.

There is a whole list of products which could be sold by enterprises to one another. There is also a list of those forbidden to be sold. Those are the very "deficit" kinds of raw materials, machinery, and instruments. Those can only be transferred through the ministry.

. . . the amount of synthetic rubber we received was strictly planned by the ministry from Moscow, but the other materials could be sent from one factory to another.

A former Gossnab official reports that enterprises can go directly to other firms for the supplies they need, depending on the kind of product, but that normally they need ministry authorization.

Managers reported on two types of contacts with other firms: formal contacts with firms designated by the ministry in the plan, and informal contacts to get deficit goods which normally are distributed by the ministry. Formal contacts specified in the plan document were established regardless of ministry affiliations and regardless of enterprise location.[9] For the most part, managers reported that officially their hands were tied: "We could not do anything directly, only through the ministry." Yet they reported informal contacts to which ministry officials "closed their eyes":

The ministry will not put me on trial for this because they also have incentive for me to fulfill the plan. It's their plan too.

. . . that was simply an illegal exchange of materials . . . no one was interested in how I acquired these materials.

Managers report that they were not encouraged to contact or trade directly with an enterprise under another ministry's jurisdiction, unless circumstances dictated the use of personal contacts to get necessary materials. In such instances, managers viewed *tolkachi* as their "direct link" with other enterprises.[10]

With one exception, managers were in agreement that all contracts must go through ministry officials.[11] The enterprises represented in this sample had no authority to establish contracts directly.

From management's perspective, adding another administrative layer in the economic bureaucracy did more to hinder than to help enterprise operation and performance. Furthermore, creating "direct links" between enterprises did not increase enterprise autonomy: firms could officially contact only those firms specified in the plan, regardless of their location and regardless of their delivery performance. Imposing sanctions for failing to meet delivery schedules was widespread, but not successful in eliminating supply problems.

V. Changes in Planning and Supply

Because general questions about the impact of the reforms on the planning process or on the supply of materials to enterprises yielded little response from informants, more specific questions were asked about changes in the planning process; whether their enterprise submitted a counterplan (*vstrechnyi plan*), for example.

Managers viewed counterplanning as an unsuccessful effort by planners to increase output; unsuccessful in large part because higher plan targets were not supported by additional supply allocations. Rather, managers were told to economize or reduce waste. Given planners' tendency to set plan targets on a percentage increase over past performance figures, managers were skeptical about the wisdom of proposing counterplans, doing so only when urged by ministry or party officials. Further, an assistant head of planning in a heavy industry enterprise reports that prior experience with planners' efforts to get enterprises to produce more dampened their enthusiasm for submitting counterplans.

Something similar happened before. The "planners" said that a portion of our profits could be used for bonuses for our workers. So our management kept careful track of materials and spending in order to maximize profits. Later, we were told: "No, it cannot be this way, you have to give your profit to the state." As in this case, there is no economic incentive. So everything reverted back to the way it was.

Informants in this sample generally concede that the reforms had no effect on the supply situation in the USSR. Supply shortages remain the number one problem management faces. These findings coincide with findings of the General Survey of the Soviet Interview Project. Of the 873 respondents asked "How often did you have supplies or equipment necessary to do your job?" 233 held positions comparable to those in the enterprise management study. That is, they held "managerial" positions in manufacturing, transportation, construction, trade and material-technical supply. As illustrated in Table 4, three-quarters of the "leaders" report significant difficulties with supply. This is in contrast to more than half of the other respondents reporting that they had sufficient supplies or equipment to do their jobs "nearly all the time."

VI. Enterprise–Ministry Relations

Western scholars know little about how the ministry functions, and even less about how its functions changed as a result of the hierarchical reforms introduced in the Soviet economic bureaucracy in the 1960s and 1970s. Over one-third of the expert informants in this sample were in contact with ministry officials during the course of their jobs; others reported on the results of such contacts by their bosses. Informants reported a wealth of information about why, when, and how they interacted with the ministry and what results obtained. But when questioned about whether the functions of the ministry changed as a result of the reforms, or whether the reforms affected enterprise-ministry relations, informants were reluctant to respond because they had little concrete information to offer. After unsuccessfully attempting with ten

Table 4

How Often Did You Have Supplies or Equipment to Do Your Job? (Soviet Interview Project: General Survey)

	Nearly always	Often	Some-times	Rarely	Never	Row total
Leaders[a]	5	3	10	10	3	31
Other managers[b]	16	3	2	2	2	25
High engineer-technical (ITR)[c]	25	10	12	7	1	55
Low ITR; other professional[d]	87	11	10	10	4	122
Column total	133	27	34	29	10	233

a. "Leaders" worked in manufacturing (8 in heavy industry, 8 in light industry and other industry), transportation (4), construction (9), and trade (22).

b. "Other managers" worked in manufacturing (4), transportation (2), construction (3), trade (14), and material-technical supply (2).

c. "High" engineer-technical personnel (ITR) worked in machine building (21), light and other industry (6), transportation (4), construction (20), and material-technical supply (1).

d. "Low" ITR and other professionals worked in manufacturing (52), transportation (5), construction (14), trade (36), and material-technical supply (4).

individuals to get some response, this question was dropped.

This finding is important because it underlines the fact that informants reported on their own work experience, unless specifically asked otherwise. What they knew, they reported with little speculation. The detailed nature of the questionnaire reduced the possibility of informants manufacturing anything beyond their own experience, making it exceedingly difficult to glorify or exaggerate their positions.

VII. Conclusions

Numerous efforts to restructure the Soviet economic bureaucracy in order to improve resource utilization and product quality appear to have had little impact on managerial decision-making at the enterprise level. Managers view reforms as ill-conceived (e.g., the Shchekino experiment caused unemployment, unequal wages for the same job, and high incomes that the state could not match with additional consumer goods; the *ob"edineniia* did not centralize supply), inadequately executed (enterprises were given more independence, but only on paper), and too frequently reversed (enterprise newly retained profits usurped by the states). From the manager's perspective, little has come of the numerous reforms: the ministry remains all-powerful, inputs are still in short supply. Consequently, management pursues plan fulfillment tactics similar to those described by Berliner (1957).[12]

As a whole, managers appear to favor more enterprise autonomy, yet remain skeptical about the ability of the leadership to focus exclusively on changes in the economic structure without corresponding changes in the political and social structure. In their view, by simply increasing the pace of the "treadmill," Gorbachev will fall far short of his goal.

Notes

1. Data for this study were produced by the Soviet Interview Project. This project was supported by Contract No. 701 from the National Council for Soviet and East European Research to the University of Illinois at Urbana-Champaign, James R. Millar, Principal Investigator. The analysis and interpretations in this study are those of the author, not necessarily of the sponsors. I thank William Moskoff for his patience and encouragement during the preparation of this manuscript.

2. Not all informants in the enterprise management project were asked the same set of questions. The open-ended questionnaire was to some extent structured, but questions were added, dropped, and reworded during the course of interviewing. I thank Gera Millar for her expert assistance with the revisions and Joe Berliner for his many valuable suggestions.

3. A full description of the Soviet Interview Project is provided by Millar (1983). For more detailed description of enterprise management study, see Linz (1986).

4. Because the General Survey and the enterprise management project were at the interview stage (in the field) at the same time, none of the respondents identified for the General Survey could be interviewed for the enterprise management study. I thank Michael Swafford and Carol Zeiss, Data Management Center, Vanderbilt University, for their assistance with the General Survey data.

5. In the machine-building industry, where each of the four occupational categories identified in Table 3 is represented, there is one instance where the findings are at odds with the general results. Seven out of ten "low" engineer-technical workers (ITR) report that labor productivity was not declining. This may reflect the sentiment expressed by engineer-technical personnel in the enterprise management sample regarding the need to produce more detailed, or more complex, designs for particular projects in the plan; or the planned reduction in number of ITR on the payroll. One informant describes the plan calling for a three percent reduction each year. Another informant reports that overfulfilling the plan resulted in a reduction in the workforce. 175

6. Participants in the enterprise management project were not asked why they chose to leave. During the course of the three-hour interview, however, several volunteered information pertaining to their decision to leave the USSR. For example, one relatively young informant felt his career had met a dead-end because he was Jewish; others explained their desire to improve career possibilities for their children.

7. For an excellent discussion of the distinction between production associations—enterprises producing a similar product brought together under one administration—and industrial associations—enterprises and R&D organizations combined, see Holmes (1981).

8. Direct links between enterprises and the goods subject to direct link supplies

are described in *Ekonomicheskaia gazeta*, no. 41 (October 1979) and no. 34 (August 1978); V.S. Kurotchenko and A.I. Baskina (eds.), *Ekonomika material'no-technicheskogo snabzheniia* (Moscow 1977), chapter 3; and V.S. Kurotchenko and K. Gyurman, *Ekonomicheskoe stimulirovanie v materl'no-technicheskom snabzhenii* (Moscow 1977).

9. For an extensive presentation of interview data pertaining to direct links, see Linz (1987b), Appendix 4b.

10. This point is highlighted in Appendix 4B in Linz (1987b).

11. An assistant director of a light industry enterprise (trained as a lawyer) reports that ''contracts between enterprises happen often and do not always need ministry's approval. It has always been like this.'' There is some possibility that he misunderstood the question.

12. I argue elsewhere (Linz 1987a) that although the nature of managerial plan fulfillment tactics remains the same, the scope was more limited in the 1970s than that portrayed by Berliner (1957).

References

Abouchar, Alan (1973). "Inefficiency and Reform in the Soviet Economy," *Soviet Studies* 25, no. 1 (July): 66–76.

Bahry, Donna (1985). "Surveying Soviet Emigrants: Political Attitudes and Ethnic Bias," unpublished manuscript, New York University (December).

Berliner, Joseph (1957). *Factory and Manager in the USSR*. Cambridge: Harvard University Press.

Campbell, Robert (1968). "Economic Reform in the USSR," *American Economic Review* (December): 547–558.

Dyker, David (1981). "Decentralization and the Command Principle—Some Lessons from Soviet Experience," *Journal of Comparative Economics*, 5, no. 2.

———— (1983). *The Process of Investment in the Soviet Union*. Cambridge: Cambridge University Press, 1983.

Hanson, Philip (1983). "Success Indicators Revisited: The July 1979 Soviet Decree on Planning and Management," *Soviet Studies* 35, no. 1 (July).

———— (1986). "The Shape of Gorbachev's Economic Reform," *Soviet Economy* 2, no. 4 (December-January): 313–26.

Hewett, Ed A. (1986). "Gorbachev at Two Years: Perspectives on Economic Development," *Soviet Economy*, 2, no. 4 (October-December): 283–88.

Holmes, Leslie (1981). *The Policy Process in Communist States: Politics and Industrial Administration*. London: Sage Publications.

Hough, Jerry F. (1986). "The Gorbachev Reform: A Maximal Case," *Soviet Economy* 2, no. 4(October-December): 302–12.

Linz, Susan J. (1986). "Emigrants as Expert-Informants on Soviet Management Decision-Making: A Methodological Note," *Comparative Economic Studies* 28, no. 3 (Fall): 65–89.

———— (1987a). "Managerial Autonomy in Soviet Firms," *Soviet Studies* (forthcoming).

———— (1987b). "The 'Treadmill' of Soviet Economic Reforms: Management's Perspective," Soviet Interview Project Working Paper, University of Illinois (August).

Millar, James R. (1983). "Emigrants as Sources of Information about the Mother Country: The Soviet Interview Project," Soviet Interview Project Working Paper, University of Illinois (December).

————— (1987). "History, Method and the Problem of Bias," in Millar (ed.), *Politics, Work and Daily Life: Survey Based on Former Soviet Citizens*. New York: Cambridge University Press (forthcoming).

Schroeder, Gertrude E. (1972). "The 'Reform' of the Supply System in Soviet Industry," *Soviet Studies* (July): 97–119.

————— (1973). "Recent Developments in Soviet Planning and Incentives," Joint Economic Committee, *Soviet Economic Prospects for the Seventies*. Washington, D.C.: US GPO, pp. 11–38.

————— (1979). "The Soviet Economy on a Treadmill of Reforms'," in Joint Economic Committee, *Soviet Economy in a Time of Change*. Washington, D.C.: US GPO, pp. 312–340.

————— (1982). "Soviet Economic Reform Decrees: More Steps on the Treadmill," in U.S. Congress, Joint Economic Committee, *Soviet Economy in the 1980s: Problems and Prospects*. Washington, D.C.: US GPO, pp. 65–88.

————— (1986). "Gorbachev: Radically Implementing Brezhnev's Reforms," *Soviet Economy* 2, no. 4 (October-December): 289–301.

About the Editors

SUSAN J. LINZ is an associate professor in the Department of Social Science at Michigan State University. She is the editor of *The Impact of World War II on the Soviet Union*.

WILLIAM MOSKOFF is the Ernest A. Johnson Professor of Economics at Lake Forest College and the editor of the journal *Comparative Economic Studies*. Professor Moskoff is the author of *Labor and Leisure in the Soviet Union: Public and Private Decision-making in a Planned Economy*.